TILING

FROM THE EDITORS OF **Fine Homebuilding**

The Taunton Press

The Taunton Press Inc., 63 South Main St., PO Box 5506, Newtown, CT 06470-5506

e-mail: tp@taunton.com

Editors: Christina Glennon and Alex Giannini

Copy editor: Diane Sinitsky

Indexer: Cathy Goddard

Cover design: Alexander Isley, Inc.

Interior design: Cathy Cassidy

Layout: David Giammattei

Front/back cover photographer: Justin Fink, courtesy *Fine Homebuilding* © The Taunton Press, Inc.

Taunton's For Pros By Pros® and *Fine Homebuilding®* are trademarks of
The Taunton Press Inc., registered in the U.S. Patent and Trademark Office.

Tiling / author, from the editors of Fine homebuilding.
    p. cm.
  Includes index.
  ISBN 978-1-60085-337-1
  1. Tile laying. I. Taunton Press. II. Fine homebuilding.
  TH8531.T56 2010
  698--dc22

                       2010042430

Printed in the United States of America

10 9 8 7 6 5 4 3 2 1

The following manufacturers/names appearing in *Tiling* are trademarks: Akemi®; Alta®; Aqua Glass®; Aquabar®; aSquare®; Better-Bench®; Chloraloy®; DensShield®; DeWalt®; Ditra® Mat; DitraSet™; Durock®; EzPoxy™; HardieBacker®; James Hardie®; Keralastic™; Laticrete®; Makita®; MAPEI®; Murphy® Oil Soap; NobleFlex®; NobleSeal® TS; Oceanside Glasstile®; Pine-Sol®; Polyblend®; Protecto® Wrap; Ridgid®; Scotch-Brite™; Schlüter®; SpectraLock® Pro; Speed® Square; Stand Off® Limestone & Marble Protector; Superior Tile Cutter®; TEC™ Super Flex™; TileLab®; Tilematic®; WonderBoard®.

About Your Safety: Homebuilding is inherently dangerous. From accidents with power tools to falls from ladders, scaffolds, and roofs, builders risk serious injury and even death. We try to promote safe work habits through our articles. But what is safe for one person under certain circumstances may not be safe for you under different circumstances. So don't try anything you learn about here (or elsewhere) unless you're certain that it is safe for you. Please be careful.

Except for new page numbers that reflect the organization of this collection, these articles appear just as they did when they were originally published. You may find that some information about manufacturers or products is no longer up to date. Similarly, building methods change and building codes vary by region and are constantly evolving, so please check with your local building department.

Special thanks to the authors, editors, art directors,
copy editors, and other staff members of *Fine Homebuilding*
who contributed to the development of the articles in this book.

CONTENTS

PART 3: TILING TECHNIQUES

INTRODUCTION

For only a few dollars per square foot, you can upgrade from an ordinary fiberglass shower to a ceramic-tiled shower surround. The inexpensive tiled shower will require more maintenance than the fiberglass and may look only marginally better. But if you can afford to kick in a few extra dollars to add a band of glass or a handful of accent tiles to the surround, you can quickly start to make the project sing. Of course, if you're not careful with your budget, you can easily blow your retirement on tile, too.

For all of these reasons, particularly its great range of style and price, tile gets a lot of coverage in *Fine Homebuilding*. It's not only a durable option for showers, either. Tile is ideal for kitchen, bathroom, and entry floors, backsplashes and countertops. Like most homebuilding projects, however, the materials you choose are only as good as the installation. Whether you're tiling over an existing laminate counter or tackling a new floor, it's the small details that make the difference between a finished project that looks good and one that looks great; one that will stain and crack and one that will last for decades to come.

For nearly 30 years we've been lucky to have tile setters like Tom Meehan and Jane Aeon share their hard-earned experiences with us. Manufacturers are helping, too. Today there are tile backerboards and membranes, mortars, thinsets, and grouts that are easy to use in every tile application. This book, a collection of the best tile stories *Fine Homebuilding* has published, is meant to help you sort through the design decisions, products, and installation details you need for a successful tile project.

Build well,

Brian Pontolilo, editor
Fine Homebuilding

Tiling a Tub Surround

■ BY MICHAEL BYRNE

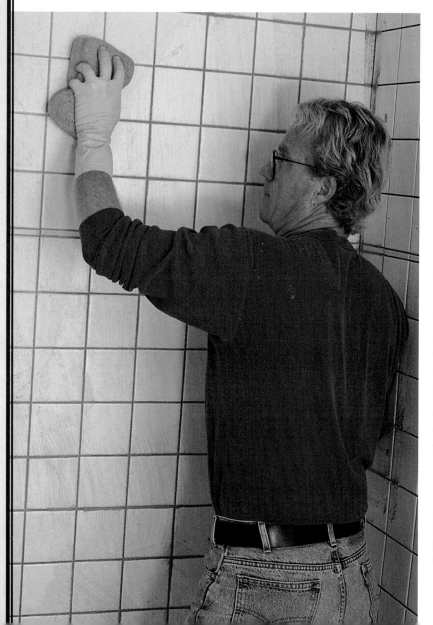

When it comes to low cost and ease of installation, it's hard to beat the fiberglass tub-and-shower unit. It's simply slid into its berth and nailed through the flanges to the framing. When the job is done, everyone gets to bathe and shower in a synthetic shell.

I prefer standard tubs enclosed by tiled walls. Tile is not only peerless in beauty and durability, but it also can be installed with minimal expertise. Whereas tub surrounds once were tiled over skillfully prepared beds of mortar, most tile pros now favor the thin-bed method. It substitutes various prefabricated backerboards for the mortar bed, saving time and trouble without compromising durability. In this chapter I'll explain how to tile a basic tub surround using the thin-bed method. The job shown is a remodel, but the principles apply to new work. To satisfy the design of the room, I did two different edge treatments, one of which mimics the look of a traditional mortar-bed surround.

Fine-tuning. After packing a wall with grout, use a damp sponge to shave high spots and fill voids.

Framing and Waterproofing

Bathtub bays must be framed plumb, level, and square using straight stock. I add extra studs and blocking to support the edges of backerboard, plus double studs to support tub enclosures, such as shower doors.

Tub surrounds need a waterproof membrane somewhere between the tile and the framing to prevent moisture infiltration. For this job, I installed economical 15-lb. asphalt felt beneath the backerboard.

Before you install felt paper, it's a good idea to mark stud locations with a crayon along the top of the tub so you'll know where to fasten the backerboard.

I staple felt to the studs or, if the framing is drywalled, I laminate the felt to the drywall with cold-patch asphalt roofing cement. Adjacent bands of felt are lapped shingle-style to shed water. For insurance, I also seal the joints with asphalt caulk and run a bead of caulk along the top edge of the tub to seal it to the paper.

If I'm working solo, I usually cut the top band of felt paper into two pieces for easier handling. If you do this, lap and seal the vertical joint to keep out water.

Start with a solid frame. Backerboard should be affixed to a sturdy and accurately framed wall that includes studs and blocking for the backerboard seams and for the tub enclosure.

Put a membrane under the backerboard. The author laps bands of 15-lb. roofing felt, stapled shingle-style to the studs, to keep moisture out of the wall. At vertical seams, he caulks the laps with asphalt to prevent leakage.

Preparing the Backerboard

I've used mesh-reinforced cement board for more than 10 years with excellent results. It has an aggregated portland-cement core with a fiberglass mesh embedded in both sides. Panels range from ¼-in. to ½-in. thick, and they come in various widths and lengths for minimal cutting and easy handling. I sometimes use ¼-in.-thick board over drywall, but I don't use board thinner than ⁷⁄₁₆ in. over bare studs because it's too flimsy.

I cut mesh-reinforced board with a carbide scriber and grind or power-sand the edges smooth. I simply mark the cutline, align the straightedge with the mark, and score the line with the scriber, making sure I cut through the mesh. Next, the board is flipped over, and the process is repeated.

Anchor the backerboard. You can use nails to affix backerboard to the studs, but the board can be damaged during installation. Corrosion-proof screws are a better choice.

Then I place a straightedge under the full length of the score, grasp the offcut, and snap it off. If the offcut is too narrow to snap, I break it off in pieces with tile biters (see "Cutting and Drilling Tiles" on p. 13).

To make small plumbing holes in mesh-reinforced board, I use a carbide-tipped hole saw. For large holes, I'll mark the opening, drill a series of ¼-in. holes around the perimeter, cut through the mesh on both sides, punch through with a hammer, and then smooth the edge of the hole with a rasp.

Installing the Backerboard

Backerboard can be hung with nails, but I prefer to use screws. They hold better than nails and put less stress on the boards during installation. I avoid regular drywall screws because their heads can snap off and because the screws can rust in a wet tub surround. I used Durock® screws (see "Sources" on p. 14) for this job. They come with a corrosion-resistant coating and built-in countersinks that help bury the heads flush with the panel.

I hang backerboard on the back wall first, then the side walls, holding the bottom course about ¼ in. off the tub to prevent water from wicking into the board and to allow room for caulk. To speed installation, I start each screw by tapping it with a hammer before I drive it home with a power screwdriver. I space the screws according to the board manufacturer's fastening schedule and provide the recommended expansion gaps around panels.

For a contemporary look, end-wall backerboard can be installed flush with adjacent drywall to allow the use of low-profile, surface-bullnose trim tiles (flat tiles with one edge rounded over). But I prefer to install the board so that it stands ½ in. proud, allowing the use of radius-bullnose trim to create the classic, curved look usually associated with mortar-bed work. To produce the

Tape the joints. Press self-adhering, fiberglass-mesh tape over the joints, applying three over-lapping strips at inside corners.

Fill tape with thinset mortar. Use a trowel to spread thinset mortar over taped joints, forcing the mortar into the fabric of the mesh.

½-in. step, you either fur out the backer-board or run drywall under it.

Backerboard joints get finished with 2-in.- or 4-in.-wide adhesive-backed fiberglass-mesh tape. In corners, I apply three overlap-ping strips of tape (see the photo above). Then I trowel the same thinset mortar over the tape that will be used for setting tiles (see the right photo above). I like to finish the joints just before I set the tiles to avoid mixing an extra batch of mortar and to avoid tiling over a thinset ridge that should have been flattened but is now a chunk of stone.

Tile Layout

The ideal layout for tiled tub surrounds produces a symmetrical appearance with minimal cutting. I start by aligning several tiles along a straightedge on the floor with a ⅛-in. spacer in each joint. Although many tiles have integral spacing lugs, they typically create a grout joint that's only 1/16 in. wide, which I think is weak looking. I like ⅛-in.-wide grout joints because they're stronger and look crisp and clean. Tile spacers—

X-shaped pieces of plastic—are available in various widths from any tile store. The num-ber of tiles represents the longest run I'll have to tile—typically the distance from the top of the tub to the ceiling. I stretch a tape from one end of the tiles and record the distance to each joint. Correlating these numbers with actual wall dimensions allows me to plan my cuts before tiling.

Back walls usually look best with identi-cal vertical rows of cut tiles at each end. I mark the vertical centerline of the wall, plumb a level to it and scribe a pencil line on the backerboard from tub to ceiling. When laying the tile, I'll work out from the centerline in both directions. End walls need one vertical line to mark the outboard edge of the field tiles. On this job, the plumbing wall would require one vertical row of cut tiles, which could be placed in the front or in the rear. Because the opposite wall would have full tiles all the way across, I chose to put full tiles in the back to match and to cut trim tiles at the front.

Instead of drawing horizontal layout lines on the wall, I level a straightedge above the rim of the tub with shims (unless the tub is

Measure the tiles. To plan tile cuts, space a row of tiles along a straightedge, measure the distance from the end of the row to each joint, and correlate the measurements with actual wall dimensions.

level enough to work off of, which is rare). I tile from the straightedge to the ceiling, remove the straightedge, and then fill in the bottom courses. Horizontal rows of cut tiles can be placed against the tub, the ceiling, or both, depending on personal preference (I put them against the ceiling on this job). They also can take the form of a decorative band somewhere in between.

Mixing and Spreading Mortar

Tiles can be bedded in mastic, but you'll get better results using thinset mortar. It's a mortar-based adhesive that's mixed with water, epoxy resin, or a liquid latex or acrylic additive that increases bond strength, compressive strength, and flexibility. I use thinset mortar mixed with 4237 liquid latex mortar additive (both made by Laticrete® International Inc.; see "Sources" on p. 14). If you're worried about fussing with too many ingredients, use a powdered thinset that includes a dry polymer additive and is mixed with water. Regardless of the mortar you use, don't mix it without donning a dust mask, safety glasses, and rubber gloves. For best results, the temperature at the job site should be between 65°F and 75°F.

Although professional installers use power mixers, the strongest mortars are mixed by

Wrong trowel. Determine the right trowel-notch size by spreading mortar on a small patch of wall. Then, comb the mortar with the trowel and firmly press the tile into the mortar. Pull the tile away and assess the coverage. There shouldn't be any bare spots. This test was done with a ¼-in. by ¼-in. trowel.

Right trowel. Minimal squeeze-out and complete coverage on the back of this tile denote a properly sized and notched trowel for applying mortar. If mortar had oozed from the edges of this test tile, the author would have switched to smaller notches. This test was done with a ¼-in. by ⅜-in. trowel.

Trowels: Square-Notch, U-Notch, or V-Notch?

The notches in these trowels determine how much tile-setting compound is distributed over a substrate. They also increase the quality of a tile's bond by eliminating voids in the compound that can lead to tile failure.

A lot of folks think that trowel choice is simply based on the type of tile-setting compound being used. However, a proper trowel should be selected based primarily on the size of the tile being used and the substrate material rather than by the type of tile-setting compound.

Square- and U-notch: different shapes but equally versatile

Although they're slightly different in shape, square- and U-notch trowels perform the same. They're best used when installing tile with mastic or thinset over rough material like cement board. However, these trowels should be used with mastic only when the specified notch depth is less than ¼ in.

Weakness: These trowels can disperse a large amount of material. Using a trowel with oversize notches, however, can lead to excess material in the grout joints that will need to be cleaned out.

V-notch: best used with small tiles on smooth substrates

V-notch trowels disperse only a small amount of compound, which makes them ideal for applying tiles smaller than 6 in. by 6 in. on smooth surfaces like drywall. These trowels are also good for applying flooring adhesives.

Weakness: The notches in these trowels don't spread thinset well because of its sand aggregate. They also don't leave behind enough material to embed large tiles or tiles with textured backs properly.

Rob Yagid is an associate editor at Fine Homebuilding.

A V-notch trowel has its niche. This tool has limited applications and even those can still be performed by a properly sized square- or U-notch trowel.

Notch depth matters as much as notch shape. The larger a tile, the deeper and wider the notch must be to obtain an adequate bond.

Spreading mortar. Use the straight edge of the notched trowel to spread thinset mortar. Use the notched edge to comb uniform ridges.

Setting the tiles. With the bottom of the tile resting on spacer blocks, the author tilts each tile onto the mortar and then presses it home.

hand. Hand mixing doesn't infuse air into the mortar as some power mixers do. I begin by pouring all of the liquid and about 75 percent of the recommended amount of thinset powder into a clean bucket. Using a margin trowel, I mix until most of the lumps are gone. Then, I add half of the remaining powder, mix, add the other half, and mix again. You have to let the material slake (rest) for 5 minutes to 10 minutes, then mix the batch once more until it's lump-free and ready to apply. The batch now should be plastic but not runny. I'm careful not to expose the mortar to direct sunlight (which can cook it) or to excessive air-conditioning (which can dry it out). At this point, the mortar should be wet enough to adhere to any surface instantly but not slip easily off the trowel.

Before applying mortar to the backerboard, I wipe the board with a damp sponge to remove dust. I apply mortar with a standard notched trowel using the smooth edge to spread the mortar on the substrate and the notched edges to comb the mortar into uniform ridges. The notch size depends on the size of the tile, the condition of the substrate, and the type of adhesive you are using. The general recommendation is to use a notch two-thirds the depth of the tile. The best way to select the proper trowel, however, is to test it with the first tile you set (see the bottom right photos on p. 8).

Setting Field Tiles

Bathtubs that are used constantly should be tiled with vitreous tiles, which are virtually waterproof. This tub is a backup, so I used standard 4¼-in. wall tiles having a soft, thin glaze and a porous, chalky bisque (the clay beneath the surface). They are less expensive than vitreous tiles, and they are easier to cut.

I tile the back wall one quadrant at a time, followed by the bottom half and top half of each end wall. Beginning at the back wall, I shim a straightedge to provide a level work surface above the tub. Then, I trowel mortar over an entire section above it (see the left photo above). I apply the mortar in a thick, relatively uniform layer, and I press hard to key it into the pores of the backerboard. That done, I comb the mortar with the notched trowel, maintaining constant contact with the board and keeping the

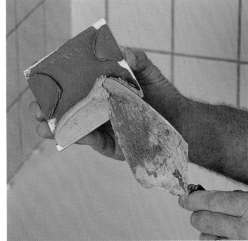

Butter the backs. For radius-bullnose trim, spread mortar on the flat part of the tile and grout on the curved part.

Look for squeeze-out. Press radius-bullnose tiles firmly enough so that grout oozes out. Remove the excess before it hardens.

Prevent sagging trim. Keep the trim tiles from drooping as they set up by taping them temporarily to the field tiles. These are surface-bullnose tiles, which are used to end a row of tile when the backerboard and the adjacent wall are in the same plane.

angle of the trowel consistent to produce ridges that are uniform.

I set the first row of tiles along the straightedge. I position the bottom edge of each tile first, then tilt it forward into the mortar (a process I call "hinging"). Then I slip a spacer between each tile, adjusting the spacing of the tiles as needed. On subsequent courses, I hinge the tiles off the spacers (see the photo at right on the facing page). I lay all full tiles in a section first, then fill in any cut tiles. If the mortar skins over before a section is finished, you should recomb it. If you break the initial set by moving a tile, scrape the mortar off the tile and the substrate and apply fresh mortar. I keep a wet sponge handy for wiping goo off the surface of tiles before it hardens.

After I've tiled all the sections on a wall and all the adhesive has set up, I remove the straightedge and install the bottom courses of tile, taping them temporarily to the tiles above to prevent sagging. Because I apply mortar carefully, I don't have to seat the tiles with the traditional beating block (a padded block of wood or plywood that's laid over tiles and rapped with a rubber mallet). Instead, I use one to coax tiles gently into a smooth plane.

To enliven this surround, I installed a liner at about eye level. A liner is a decorative horizontal stripe of tile, usually less than 1 in. wide, that's used to interrupt a field of tiles. Stock liners are available in unlimited sizes and colors, but I cut my own out of matching or slightly contrasting field and trim

Nibble the notches. Use a biter to notch tiles around plumbing, working in from the corners of the notch to prevent unwanted breakage.

tiles. In some cases, liners can eliminate the need to install horizontal rows of cut tiles against the ceiling or tub.

Setting Trim Tiles

Surface-bullnose trim tiles are cut and installed just as field tiles, then temporarily taped to neighboring tiles to prevent sagging (see the left photo on p. 11). To install radius-bullnose trim tiles, I apply a skin coat of thinset mortar to the backerboard and to the flat part of the tile backs. Then, I butter the curves on the tile backs with the same grout I use for tile joints (see the top right photo on p. 11). A small amount of grout should squeeze out the ends of each tile as I push it home (see the bottom right photo on p. 11). I lay the whole row, then nudge it into alignment with a straightedge, gently tapping the tiles flat with the trowel handle and applying tape to prevent sagging. When the grout begins to solidify, I pare the edge square to the drywall with the margin trowel.

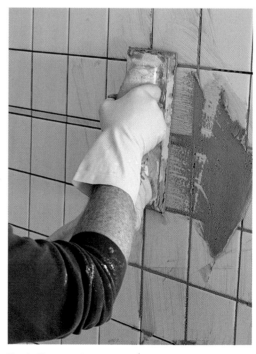

Pack the grout. Hold the trowel at a slight angle and spread grout over a small section. Work grout into the joints until they are full.

Ready for grout. Load freshly mixed grout onto the rubber face of a grout trowel.

Cutting and Drilling Tiles

The snap cutter, which you can rent from many tile stores and tool-rental shops, is the tool to use for cutting tiles down to ½ in. wide. I mark cutlines on the tiles with a fine-point, felt-tip pen, then score and break the tiles with the cutter. I then ease the resulting sharp edges with a tile-rubbing stone.

Biters are used primarily for trimming tiles to fit around plumbing (see the top photo on the facing page). They have a curved cutting edge on one side and a straight one on the other that bites into the glazed side of the tile. To make holes in the middle of tiles, I use a carbide-tipped hole saw.

For removing less than ½ in. from tiles, you have to score the tiles with the snap cutter, then nibble to the line with a pair of biters, working in from the corners of the tiles to prevent breakage. And, again, you would smooth the raw edges with a rubbing stone. To make a tile less than ½ in. wide requires a wet saw.

Grouting

Tile spacers come in various thicknesses, and some are thin enough that you can grout right over them. I prefer the thicker spacers, and I pull them out (using a dental pick) after the thinset cures. Once I've removed all the tile spacers and globs of thinset mortar from the joints, I'm ready to grout. I check the thinset container to see if there's a waiting period. If so, I wait, or the thinset mortar might stain the grout.

I use a powdered polymer-modified grout called Polyblend® from Custom Building Products (see "Sources" on p. 14), which is mixed with water. It comes in 47 colors, and the company sells caulks to match.

Only the rubber face of a grout trowel can pack joints full without scratching tiles (see the bottom left photo on the facing page). I start with the back wall and use the trowel to spread grout over a small section. I tilt the trowel to a 40-degree angle or less and work the grout into the joints (see the bottom right photo on the facing page). I attack

Remove the excess. Hold the trowel nearly perpendicular to the wall and scrape off the excess grout with the edge of the trowel.

Wet cleanup. Complete wet cleaning by making parallel strokes with a damp sponge, using a clean side of the sponge per wipe.

Sources

Custom Building Products
800-272-8786
www.custombuilding
products.com
Polyblend

Laticrete International Inc.
800-243-4788
www.laticrete.com
Thinset mortar and
4237 liquid latex mortar
additive

Miracle Sealants Co.
800-350-1901
www.miraclesealants.com
511 Impregnator

USG
800-874-4968
www.usg.com
Durock screws

joints from three directions, with each pass cramming more grout into the joint until it's completely filled. Once all the joints in a section are filled, I hold the trowel at a right angle to the surface and rake it diagonally along the tiles to scrape off excess grout (see the bottom left photo on p. 13). I grout the entire wall this way, packing everything except for the expansion joint above the tub and gaps around plumbing fixtures. Because grout will stiffen in the bucket, it should be stirred occasionally.

Next, I thoroughly wring out a wet, rounded sponge and gently wipe the freshly packed wall in a circular motion to shave off high spots. I avoid feathering the grout over the edges of the tiles. Then, I complete the wet cleaning by making 3-ft.-long parallel swipes with the damp sponge, using a clean face for each swipe (see the bottom right photo on p. 13). At this point, I rinse the sponge after every two swipes.

About 15 minutes later, grout haze should be visible on the surface of the tile. I remove it by rubbing the tiles with a soft cloth or cheesecloth. If that doesn't work, I'll try a damp sponge or white Scotch-Brite™ pad.

At this stage, with the grout set up, I use a utility knife to remove the grout from the corner joint and from the ¼-in. joint I left between the tile and the tub. These expansion joints need to be filled with sealant.

After all grouting and cleaning is completed, I let the job rest while the grout cures and dries (usually about 72 hours). Then, I return to seal the grout and the raw edges of the tile with an impregnator. I use 511 Impregnator made by the Miracle Sealants Company (see "Sources" at left). You have to allow the impregnator to dry before you caulk the expansion joints around the tub. I use a sealant that can be color matched to the tile, the grout, or the plumbing fixture.

Michael Byrne is the author of Setting Tile, *published by The Taunton Press, Inc.*

Dry cleanup. About 15 minutes after sponging, wipe off grout haze with a dry cloth, leaving the surround ready for sealing and caulking.

Upgrading to a Tile Shower

■ BY TOM MEEHAN

When fiberglass shower units were first introduced in the 1970s, they were the stars of the plumbing world. Inexpensive and relatively easy to install, they didn't crack and were easy to clean. Fiberglass units had their own problems, but they worked.

These days, bathrooms are a big renovation target for many homeowners, who might not know how to deal with their old fiberglass tub/shower units (see the photo below). For this project, I removed the old tub unit in pieces, did a little carpentry, and

Work from the top down. The first cuts are made in the corners to separate the unit's walls from the tub.

It takes only a few cuts. Once the walls are removed, the tub should come out in pieces that are small enough to cart away without scratching walls and woodwork (below).

Time to call a plumber. The plumber levels the drain (left) so that it matches the shower-pan floor. He also replaces the mixing valve with a thermostatic pressure-balanced shower valve (below).

had a plumber relocate the drain and mixing valve. After that, the job was like any other: a site-built pan, backerboard substrate, and tile (in this case limestone) combined with some interesting details that made a luxurious shower (see the right photo on p. 15).

Demolition: The Fun Stage with Quick Results

To take out the existing shower unit, I first shut off the main water valve to the house, then start disassembling the plumbing fixtures (mixing valve and shower head, etc.). The door is closed and the fan turned on to keep dust out of the house. I always cut the drywall along the outside edge of the unit with a knife, hammer, and chisel to avoid damaging the drywall outside the shower stall.

Next, I put on a dust mask and safety glasses, stick a new wood-cutting blade in a reciprocating saw, and start cutting from the top, working down. It helps to have someone hold some of the loose pieces, which vibrate as they are cut free from the rest of the unit.

Tile Backerboard: HardieBacker, Durock, and DensShield

Backerboard panels provide a flat, firm base for the installation of tile. They are resistant to the effects of water exposure, including swelling, rot, and mold growth, and they can be used in fire-resistant assemblies. Each type of backerboard costs roughly the same and is available in similar dimensions at most lumberyards. However, each has characteristics that affect where it can be installed and how tile is placed on it.

HardieBacker®

Composition: Hardie-Backer is made of cellulose fibers that are layered with cement slurry and cured through high-pressure autoclaving. The boards are also infused with additives to inhibit mold growth.

Weight: 2.6 lb. per sq. ft. (½ in. thick)

Mortar: Modified latex thinset should be used on HardieBacker. This type of thinset is more expensive than nonmodified products and also sets up faster—a benefit when working with large, heavy tile.

Installation: HardieBacker is best cut with carbon-tipped sawblades or specialty cutting shears and fastened to studs or joists with 1½-in. corrosion-resistant screws or nails.

Notes: HardieBacker has a smooth surface that allows the panel to be finished with products other than tile, including wallpaper and paint. This makes the panels useful for finished basements or garages that would benefit from the panels' moisture protection.

Durock

Composition: Durock panels have an aggregated portland-cement core and are wrapped with a polymer-coated, glass-fiber mesh.

Weight: 3 lb. per sq. ft. (½ in. thick)

Mortar: Tile can be set with modified latex thinset or nonmodified dry-set mortar. The latter is a less expensive option with a longer working time.

Installation: Durock is best cut with carbon-tipped sawblades or specialty cutting shears and fastened to studs or joists with 1½-in. corrosion-resistant screws or nails.

Notes: Unlike other backerboard, Durock meets industry standards for resistance to freeze/thaw cycles, allowing it to be used in exterior applications.

DensShield®

Composition: Dens-Shield is a blend of glass fibers and gypsum sandwiched between two fiberglass mats. The front of the panel is faced with an acrylic coating that acts as a moisture barrier.

Weight: 2 lb. per sq. ft. (½ in. thick)

Mortar: As with HardieBacker, modified latex thinset should be used to set tile on Dens-Shield panels.

Installation: DensShield can be cut with the same tools suggested for HardieBacker and Durock, or it can be scored and snapped like regular drywall. DensShield can be fastened to studs and joists with 1½-in. corrosion-resistant screws or nails.

Notes: Unlike other backerboard, DensShield can't be used where extreme levels of heat and moisture are common, such as in saunas or steam rooms.

Rob Yagid is an associate editor at Fine Homebuilding.

Each piece that's carted away makes it easier to attack the remaining section; usually the unit comes out in five or six pieces. The hardest piece to remove surrounds the drain; here, practicing a little patience and cutting smaller pieces help. Once I've cut out around the drain, I reach down and undo the drain assembly with a wrench.

Relocating the Drain for the New Pan

Once the old tub is removed, the drain typically must be moved from the tub end to the center of the new shower pan. After I open the subfloor, the plumber can reroute the drain and vent to the new position (see the drawing on p. 20).

Backerboard Creates a Water-Resistant Substrate

Unlike moisture-resistant gypsum-based products, cementitious backerboard can't come apart, even if it's soaking wet. Unless the installation is for a commercial steam shower, I don't use a vapor barrier between the framing and the backerboard. My experience tells me that any water vapor that does end up in the stud bays won't react with the backer or thinset and will evaporate quickly.

I make sure to use the largest pieces possible. Fewer pieces equals fewer joints, which minimizes any potential for water problems. I attach the backerboard with 1½-in. galvanized roofing nails or screws, and don't put any fasteners lower than 2 in. above the threshold to avoid leaks.

Securing the backerboard. The author likes to nail the substrate every 6 in. to 8 in. (see the photo at right). All seams are then sealed with fiberglass-mesh tape bedded in thinset and troweled smooth (see the photo at far right).

Don't Forget to Change the Vent Location

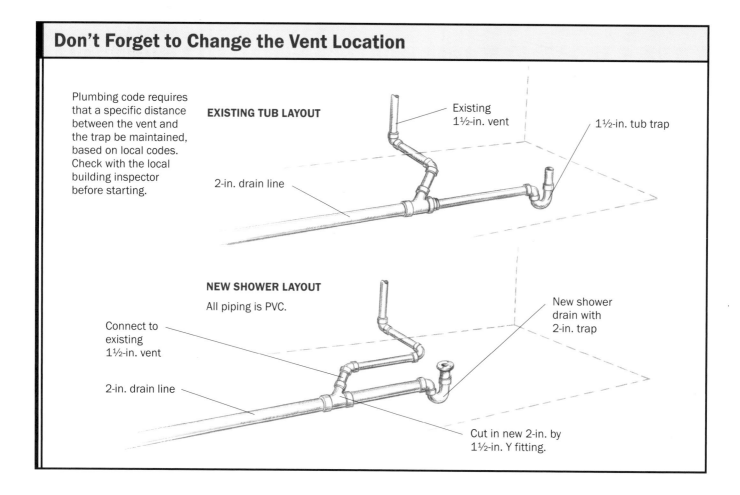

Plumbing code requires that a specific distance between the vent and the trap be maintained, based on local codes. Check with the local building inspector before starting.

EXISTING TUB LAYOUT

Existing 1½-in. vent

1½-in. tub trap

2-in. drain line

NEW SHOWER LAYOUT

All piping is PVC.

New shower drain with 2-in. trap

Connect to existing 1½-in. vent

2-in. drain line

Cut in new 2-in. by 1½-in. Y fitting.

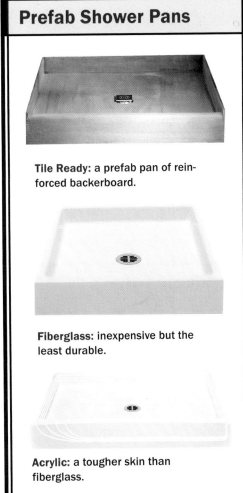

Tile Ready: a prefab pan of reinforced backerboard.

Fiberglass: inexpensive but the least durable.

Acrylic: a tougher skin than fiberglass.

Sources

American Standard
800-442-1902
www.americanstandard-us.com
Acrylic/fiberglass
shower pans

Aqua Glass®
800-632-0911
www.aquaglass.com

Aquatic
800–877-2005
www.aquaticbath.com

Georgia-Pacific
800-225-6119
www.gp.com
DensShield

Innovis Corporation
916-361-2601
www.innoviscorp.com
Better-Bench®, galvanized-steel seat form

James Hardie®
888-JHARDIE
www.jameshardie.com
HardieBacker

Laticrete
International Inc.
800-243-4788
www.laticrete.com
Thinsets

Noble Company
800-878-5788
www.noblecompany.com
Chlorinated polyethylene waterproof membrane

Pro Spec/Bonsal
American
800-334-0784
www.prospec.com

USG
800-874-4968
www.usg.com
Durock

Shower Pans: Build Your Own or Buy Them Ready Made

I like to build my shower pans with a waterproof membrane and built up mud floor (see the photo above). I think this type of pan makes the best substrate for a tile floor because it's solid, won't crack, and can conform to fit any space.

But if you want something faster, you can buy a prefab pan that you still can tile over. Made of waterproof extruded polystyrene and backerboard, these pans have floors that slope uniformly to a built-in drain and are relatively easy to install.

A shower doesn't always have to have a tiled floor and threshold; often, a homeowner just wants a simpler look. Options include prefab shower pans made of fiberglass and acrylic that look fine with most tile jobs (see the sidebar above). They come in standard sizes that fit many, but not all, installations and are found in most plumbing-supply houses and home centers.

__Tom Meehan__ is a second-generation tile installer who has been installing tile for more than 35 years. Tom lives with his wife, Lane, and their four sons in Harwich, Massachusetts, where they own Cape Cod Tileworks.

The Details: Make a Tile Shower Sparkle

The difference between an average tile job and an outstanding one is often a matter of a few relatively inexpensive details that don't require lots of time but can really personalize the bath area.

SHAMPOO SHELF

When laying out the shampoo shelf, first determine where the full tiles will land to keep tile cuts to a minimum. A vacuum helps remove dust as the backerboard is cut.

SOAP DISH

The author installed a little limestone soap dish into notches cut across the tops of two tiles. (If you're using ceramic tile, solid-surface material works, too.) He squared up the corners and sanded down the front edge, then cut three 2-in.-long slots for a drain.

DECORATIVE BORDER

Used for an accent, small mesh-backed tiles are easier to install if they're first mounted on a piece of waterproof membrane with binding-fortified thinset. The membrane also brings the small tiles flush with the big ones.

CORNER SEAT

Available in different sizes (see "Sources" on p. 21), the galvanized-steel seat form is screwed into the framing behind the backerboard at a height of 18 in. from the floor.

2 Remove the waste, then reinforce the opening with 2x scrap material secured to the backerboard with construction adhesive and galvanized screws.

3 After coating the recess with thinset, cover the inside with a piece of water-proof membrane, folding and sealing corners as needed. Prefab inserts are also available.

4 Starting with the bottom piece, line the recess with tile, followed in order by the back, top, and sides. All pieces should be back coated with a layer of thinset.

2 The next day, when the thinset has dried, the assembly is cut into uniform strips two tiles wide and to a length that matches the width of the large tiles.

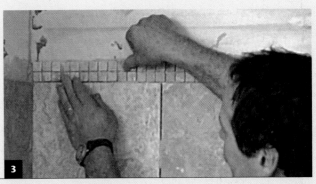

3 The strips now can be applied to the backerboard with a liberal coating of thinset.

2 The form then is filled with mud, which creates the substrate for the tile. After the top is leveled off, the mud is left to dry overnight.

3 After the mud is prepped with successive layers of thinset, waterproof membrane, and thinset, tile is laid across the top, then the front. Temporary braces keep the edge tile in place until the thinset bonds.

Installing a Shower Niche

■ BY JANE AEON

Tired of bumping into that wire shower caddy hanging awkwardly off the showerhead? Do you hate the unsightly clutter at the edges of your bathtub? Organize your shower or bath space by building a niche that offers convenient storage and a charming sense of bathroom design. In recent years, these small recessed spaces have become popular components of bathtub surrounds and showers. In fact, all the bathrooms I tile these days are outfitted with some sort of niche.

Niche Size and Location Affect Function

Before determining where on the wall the niche should go, decide the size that would be most useful for your shower niche. I often build 12-in. by 12-in. niches, but I find that 14-in.-tall niches can accommodate oversize shampoo bottles a little better. Don't let standard stud spacing be the sole determinant in the size of a niche. The benefit of building a niche, as opposed to installing a prefabricated one (see the sidebar on p. 29), is that you can easily create spaces of all shapes and sizes.

Determine the Location of the Niche with a Story Pole

By modifying the framing in a bathroom wall with blocking, you can build custom-size niches in almost any location on the wall. First, though, create a story pole (I use my aluminum straightedge) by marking off tiles spaced for ¼-in. grout joints. Held vertically against the wall, this layout tool helps to determine where to frame the niche by ensuring that it won't be bordered by awkwardly sized tiles.

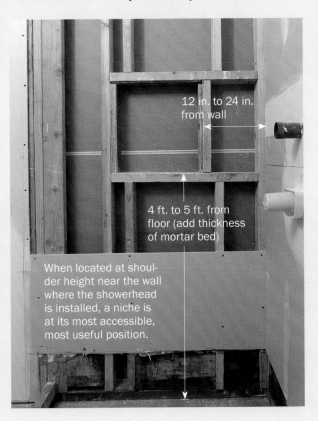

12 in. to 24 in. from wall

4 ft. to 5 ft. from floor (add thickness of mortar bed)

When located at shoulder height near the wall where the showerhead is installed, a niche is at its most accessible, most useful position.

Once you've decided on the size of the niche and a general location on the wall that balances accessibility and aesthetics, fine-tune its position with a story pole to be sure that the niche opening lines up with the grout joints. Transfer the layout marks from the story pole to the studs to orient the framing of the niche and then again on the backerboard once it's installed to guide the tile layout.

In the project featured here, the architect and builder positioned and framed the niche slightly above the height of a nearby vanity. I had to increase the width of the grout joints so that the tiles would align properly on the wall.

Frame the Niche Larger than Necessary

To frame most niche openings, I nail horizontal 2x blocking between the existing studs. But each installation has subtle differences.

Flash the Wall and Niche to Prevent Water Intrusion

In many parts of the country, greenboard drywall doesn't meet code for use as a tile substrate due to its poor performance in wet conditions. Here, I use it behind cement backerboard, which meets code, as a means of building out the shower wall. I then can install an attractive quarter-round edge tile at the thickened edge of the shower, where the tile ends and the wallboard begins. Its use, however, puts an even stronger emphasis on proper waterproofing measures.

Flexible flashing seals the niche

I place a thin, self-adhesive flexible-flashing membrane in the niche, being sure to lap each strip at least an inch over the one below so that any water is shed down the wall rather than being trapped inside it (photo 1). I like Protecto® Wrap (see "Sources" on p. 29) flexible flashing because it's easy to work with, and like other flexible flashings, it seals securely around nail and staple penetrations.

A vapor retarder keeps the framing and wallboard dry

I use Fortifiber's Aquabar® (see "Sources" on p. 29), which is two layers of kraft paper laminated with asphalt. I attach it directly to the face of the greenboard or studs with staples (photo 2), making sure to double-layer each corner for added protection. The bottom strip of niche flashing should lap over the vapor retarder (photo 3).

Caulk seals both membranes

I cut out the niche opening and seal the edges with silicone caulk (photo 4) before securing them with staples.

Line the Niche with Backerboard and Mud

Creating a solid, uniform substrate is crucial. After cutting and screwing ½-in. cement backerboard to the wall, I line the top, back, and sides of the niche with scraps. Mudding the bottom is the last preparation step.

Don't screw in the niche's back panel

Measure, cut, and place a few beads of silicone caulk on the back of the niche's back panel prior to installing it. This piece is also held in place by the pressure of the niche's top and side pieces, which are secured with screws.

Tape all the joints at once

Once all the backerboard is firmly in place, I cover each joint in the shower with mesh tape and a coat of thinset. When the thinset has cured, I knock down any imperfections and high spots with a sanding block.

Slope the bottom to shed water

Trowel a ½-in. layer of mortar in the bottom of the niche, and use a level to make sure it has a slight pitch. Slant the bottom of the niche just enough so that water flows out of it, but not so much that bars of soap and bottles of shampoo slide out. I aim for a ⅛-in. slope over 3 in.

Story Pole Keeps Tile Layout on Course

On a typical project, the tile layout is determined when I first begin framing the niche. I use the story pole as a reference to draw layout lines on the wall. Then I lay tile as I would on any other vertical tiling project.

1 Transfer layout marks to the wall

I make layout marks on each side of the niche with a mechanical pencil for absolute accuracy.

1. Mark both the top and bottom locations of each course of tile, not just one edge.

2. Use a 4-ft. level to connect and extend the layout marks on each side of the niche.

3. Complete the layout lines within the niche by using a small level.

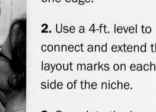

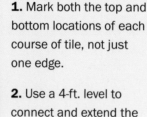

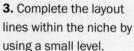

Secure top tiles with short sticks

Thanks to careful layout, the niche lands nicely in the tiled shower wall. To hold up the niche's top tiles while the thinset cures, I wedge two vertical pieces of scrap wood under one flat, horizontal piece.

In some 2x4 walls, the existing framing is shallower than 3½ in. In these cases, I use ¼-in.-thick backerboard in the back of the niche instead of ½-in.-thick backerboard to gain as much usable space as possible. When working with a 2x6 wall, I have to choose between creating a deep recess or padding it out with plywood or backerboard to decrease its depth.

No matter what type of framing you have to deal with, always frame the niche at least ¾ in. to 1 in. larger than you want the final opening to be. This allows you to adjust the tile layout if necessary and also provides room for ⅛-in.-thick waterproofing membrane, ½ in. of mortar and backerboard, and the thickness of the tile. If you're using quarter-round edge tiles, like in this bath, give yourself even more room; this type of tile requires a bit more space.

A Hole in a Wet Wall Can be Disastrous

If you're not intimidated by installing a shower niche, you should be. You're creating a hole in a wall located in the wettest area of your home. Poorly flashing and waterproofing this recess can easily lead to mold and rot problems.

In this bathroom, the architect specified quarter-round edge tiles around the niche and along the edges of the shower. To accommodate this detail, I attached backerboard over greenboard to fur out the shower perimeter from the bathroom wall. Otherwise, I would attach the backerboard directly to the studs. I use three waterproofing products in and around niches (see the photos on p. 26), and their installation is the same with each type of wall assembly.

Create a Solid Substrate in the Niche

I like using standard cement backerboard in bathrooms because tiles don't set up on it nearly as quickly as with fiber-cement backerboard. That means I can make minor adjustments to the tile as I go. However, I usually use whatever product that I have excess of to avoid wasting material.

When installing backerboard in a shower niche, I install the back panel with silicone, not screws. By using silicone, I eliminate the possibility of damaging the drywall on the opposite side of the bathroom wall.

Once the cement backerboard is in place, I cover all the joints with mesh tape buried in thinset. I finish the mud work by troweling a ½-in. layer of mortar in the bottom of the niche, slightly sloped to the outside edge so that water can drain from the niche instead of pooling inside it.

Lay Tile as if Working on a Regular Wall

Tiling a wall with a well-appointed niche is done like any other wall-tiling project. When working in the shower niche, I install a row of tiles on the bottom of the niche first, followed by a course of tiles in the back of the niche; these tiles are held flush to the tops of the bottom tiles. Applying the niche's side tiles and edge treatment, if called for, completes the course.

In some bathrooms, I like to replace the bottom tiles with a piece of solid stone for a dramatic yet elegant look. The installation sequence is the same, but the visual interest is certainly not.

Jane Aeon is a tile contractor in Berkeley, California and Oklahoma City, Oklahoma.

Sources

Ceramic Tile Specialties
704-957-8594
www.getproform.com
Prefab niche

Fortifiber Building Systems Group
800-773-4777
www.fortifiber.com

Innovis Corporation
916-361-2601
www.innoviscorp.com
Prefab niche

Noble Company
800-878-5788
www.noblecompany.com
Prefab niche

Protecto Wrap Company
800-759-9727
www.protectowrap.com

Prefab Niches Have Their Place

I often use prefabricated niches when a homeowner or architect calls for a more elaborate design. There's simply no other way to get a niche with a steepled or arched top secured into a wall as quickly.

Prefabricated niches (see "Sources" above right) eliminate some of the steps called for when framing a niche from scratch. There's no need to mortar the bottom of the niche because prefab niches have a slope built into their form. There are fewer joints to tape and mud, and waterproofing measures are generally less stringent because prefab niches are solid, one-piece units.

However, prefabricated niches have some limitations. Installation of certain models can be finicky if a wall's framing is warped or out of square. And although these niches come in a variety of sizes, they don't offer nearly as much adjustability with regard to tile layout as a framed niche.

Prefab niches

Tiling a Shower with Marble

■ BY TOM MEEHAN

Back a few hundred million years or so, Earth was working overtime. Incredible forces and pressures within the planet moved continents and created mountains. Limestone, formed from the skeletons and shells of countless sea creatures, underwent an intense and miraculous transformation during this period. The result of this metamorphosis is marble, which has become a prized building material.

While marble was being formed, various minerals and contaminants were introduced, producing the veins and rich colors that make each batch of marble unique. However, all of these wonderful colors make installing marble an interesting challenge. In 25 years as a tile installer, I have learned the importance of opening every box of marble and shuffling the tiles to get the veins and colors to work together before a project begins. My goal is to blend the tiles in such a way that the finished shower wall resembles a solid slab of marble.

The project in this article is a 7-ft. by 3½-ft. shower stall with a built-in seat and a shampoo shelf. The shower-door enclosure runs the full 7 ft. along the front of the shower bay with 1-ft. returns on both ends (see the photo on the facing page). This arrangement shows off the entire expanse of marble. For this particular shower, my clients chose green marble, which needs special treatment because of its chemical makeup. Green-marble tile reacts negatively to all cement based thinsets, both water-based and acrylic, causing the tile to warp and break down (see "Green Marble, Proceed with Caution" on p. 32). I avoid these problems by sealing the back of each tile with epoxy before it is installed, which I will describe in detail later on.

Backerboard Must Be Kept off the Floor

Marble tiles for any shower should be mounted on cement backerboard. For this project I used Durock (see "Sources" on p. 37), which consists of a thin layer of cement sandwiched between two layers of fiberglass mesh.

Even though backerboard is not supposed to deteriorate or fall apart, it is a porous material and must be kept off the bottom of the shower floor to prevent moisture from wicking up the wall (see the top photo on p. 32). If the backerboard gets wet, it can stain the marble tile from behind.

A showy shower out of stone. Before installation, marble tiles are arranged so that the veins and colorations all work together. The tiles are put on as flat as possible and tight to one another to give the impression of a solid slab of marble.

Green Marble, Proceed with Caution

Installing green marble can be a disaster if not done properly. In fact, it should probably only be attempted by a qualified professional. Almost all green marble reacts to cement-based thinsets. In the first six hours, the marble starts to cup, which means the outside edges curl up a little. While the marble will usually return to its original form after six hours, the bond can break where the tile curled.

Because of this reaction, most adhesive manufacturers recommend that green marble be set directly on the wall with epoxy. While this is an option, there are some drawbacks to this method. Using epoxy as the complete bonding agent with no other thinset involved is expensive. Also, epoxy is difficult to work with. It sags and cannot be built up like thinset cement, and, if the walls are a little uneven, it will be difficult to plane out.

The method demonstrated in this chapter combines both epoxy and thinset, which prevents the tile from curling and allows for an easier and less expensive installation. When the tile has been back-buttered with epoxy the day before, as in this chapter, the very best latex-modified thinset must be used to bond to the epoxy, such as MAPEI® Keralastic™, Laticrete 333, or TEC™ Super Flex™ (see "Sources" on p. 37). It is essential to follow manufacturer recommendations for all products involved. Be sure to pay attention because each company may have different specs. When thinset is applied to the wall, it must also be skim-coated onto the backside of the green marble where the epoxy was applied the day before. This is called burnishing, and it is the only way to have 100% contact.

I usually keep it around 1½ in. from the floor. I also keep the nails in my backerboard above the top of the shower pan or at least 5 in. from the floor to prevent the shower pan from leaking. Installing the backerboard too low and nailing through the shower pan are probably the two most frequent causes of failure with a marble-tile installation in a shower.

Cutting and installing the backerboard is a lot like hanging drywall, except that all of my straight cuts are done with a special backerboard knife with a carbide blade. These knives are available at your local tile or big-box store. I treat backerboard the same as a piece of drywall, making three or four long

Keeping the backerboard off the floor will save headaches later. A 2x4 block is used as a spacer to hold the backerboard off the shower floor. If installed too low, backerboard can soak up moisture that will stain the marble from behind.

A hammer works like a hole saw. The quickest, easiest way to make a hole in backerboard is to pulverize the unwanted cement by tapping it with a hammer. A utility knife can be used to cut the mesh away from both sides of the board.

strikes along a straightedge and then bending the sheet back and slicing the mesh on the back with a utility knife. For cutting right angles or corners, I use my grinder with a 4-in. diamond blade. Grinder cutting creates a lot of dust, so I wear a respirator and try to cut outside whenever possible.

Small holes in backerboard can be drilled with a carbide-tipped hole saw. But large holes for the mixing valve and pipes are made a little differently (see the bottom photo on the facing page). First I map out where I want the board removed. Then I tap at the board with a hammer until the area inside my lines has been reduced to cement dust with just the mesh on both sides holding it in place. At this point, I cut away the mesh with a utility knife and remove the pulverized cement.

Before installing the board, I check the studs with a straightedge to make sure they are all in the same plane. If need be, I build out any studs that are out of line to keep the backerboard as flat as possible. The backerboard gets nailed to the wall every 8 in. with 1½-in. galvanized ring-shank nails. I also put in a few galvanized screws along the seams for extra reinforcement. With the board nailed in place, I finish the seams with mesh tape and thinset mortar to seal the joints and prevent future cracking and settling.

Green Marble Needs to Be Sealed with Epoxy before Installation

Most marble can be put directly on the wall with regular thinset mortar, but as I mentioned before, green marble is apt to warp and break down. Adhesive manufacturers recommend that green marble be set directly on the wall with epoxy mortar, but this procedure requires large quantities of epoxy, which is very expensive. A different solution that I've used successfully is sealing the

Epoxy seals the backs of the green-marble tiles. Green marble reacts badly to water-based adhesives, so the backs of the tiles are sealed with nonporous epoxy. A trowel spreads the thick and gooey epoxy.

backs of the green-marble tiles with epoxy and installing them with thinset, which is less expensive than epoxy, mixed with the proper additive (see the photo above).

I use an epoxy product made by Laticrete International Inc. (see "Sources" on p. 37). The three-part mixture comes conveniently in a can with a pair of disposable gloves and a white scrub pad for warm-water cleanup. Working with epoxy is something akin to working with saltwater taffy—sticky, messy, and tedious. So I make an extra effort to keep this part of the operation as neat and orderly as possible. Using a flat trowel, I skim-coat the back of each tile with a thin layer of epoxy. Then I stand the tiles upright and on edge to dry, just barely touching each other.

After giving the epoxy 24 hours to dry, I scrape all of the tiles' edges with a sharp utility knife to remove any excess. Cleaning the edges will ensure that the tiles will fit together tightly when they are installed.

Once the backs of the marble tiles have been coated with epoxy, the proper thinset must be used to bond the tiles to the walls and floor. Plain thinset or thinset with a

basic acrylic additive is fine for regular marble and might seem to work initially for the epoxy-coated tiles as well. But the longevity of a bond between regular thinset and epoxy is questionable. The thinset must be mixed with an additive specifically designed for bonding to a resilient surface such as vinyl or linoleum flooring. This mixture will also bond to the nonporous epoxy coating on the marble. MAPEI and Laticrete both make good products for this application (see "Sources" on p. 37).

A Ledger Board Starts the Tiles Out Level

The two main objectives when installing marble tile are keeping the joints between tiles tight and making the walls a continuous, flat, even plane.

I took great pains ahead of time to build this shower stall in even 12-in. increments. This careful planning kept my cut tiles close to full size. I laid out the shower with full-width tile for the top course against the ceiling and cut tile on the bottom course along the floor. Rather than begin my tile installation with the cut course, however, I opted to start with the first course of full-width tiles. To keep this starter course

A ledger board keeps the starter course level. A length of 1x is leveled and tacked to the wall to provide support and alignment for the starting course of tile.

Thinner tiles are used to build out the decorative band. Full-size tiles are cut into smaller squares, then cut in half again. A complementary color was chosen for the diamond. Instead of giving these smaller tiles a thick bed of mortar, thin and unglazed tiles were used to shim them out to the plane of the rest of the wall.

perfectly level, I tacked a ledger board on the wall along the bottom edge of the course of tile (see the top photo on the facing page). This ledger board also provided some support for the heavy marble tiles while the adhesive was curing.

I began by spreading my thinset mixture on the walls with a ⅜-in. notched trowel, covering enough of the wall for two courses. Then I buttered the back of each tile before it went on the wall. With this amount of thinset, I can push a tile in or build it out as needed to keep the wall perfectly flat. Two tools that come in handy for this process are a rubber mallet and a large suction cup with a release switch, available at tile stores, glass shops, or marble-supply stores. I use the mallet to tap tiles in and to keep them tight to one another, and the suction cup lets me pull a tile out and reset it if it's in too far. Keep in mind that, unlike ceramic tile, marble has a square outside edge that becomes visible with the slightest bit of unevenness in the installation. After setting the first three courses on the back wall, I moved to the side walls to give the thinset a chance to set a little before adding the weight of the additional courses.

Simple Cuts and a Complementary Color Create a Decorative Border

To minimize the cold, formal look a large marble shower stall can sometimes have, my client decided to add a decorative band just above the fifth course of tile (see the photo on p. 31). To create this border, I used my wet saw to cut a bunch of the sealed green tiles and several beige marble tiles into 4-in. squares. Then I cut each of the 4-in. green tiles in half diagonally and created a two-tone diamond band that runs around the perimeter of the shower. At the corners of the shower stall, I used half of a beige diamond going in both directions to give the appearance of a folded tile.

Building these small tiles out to the same plane as the rest of the wall can present a problem. I had used a fairly thick layer of adhesive to keep the 12-in. by 12-in. tiles flat. This method can get pretty sloppy and difficult when building out small tiles. So I used some leftover unglazed mosaic tiles as shims to bring the decorative pieces out flush with the field tiles (see the bottom photo on the facing page). The thinset adhesive had no problem adhering to mosaic tile because both sides of the tile were unglazed.

Bullnosing the Tiles Can Be Done with a Saw and a Grinder

I bullnosed, or rounded the edges of, all of the tiles for the outside corners of the shower stall to soften the edge. I own a water-fed router, but it was in the repair shop when I was working on this project. Because the router is both wet and loud, I try to use it only if I have a lot of bullnosing to do. Instead of the router, I used another method that's a bit slower and requires a little more patience. But I find it gives the same great results.

First I run a tile through my tile saw, holding it at a 45-degree angle, removing only about ⅛ in. from the edge of the tile. After making this cut on several tiles, I set up five or six in a row on the edge of a table or bench. I use a grinder or spin sander with 80-grit paper to round off the two edges of the chamfer and create the bullnose on all five tiles at once. Then I polish the rounded edge with sanding disks, working progressively up to 600 grit.

Diamond pads soaked in water can also be used to create the bullnose after chamfering. These pads make less dust and work better on marble than regular sanding disks. Diamond pads come as a six-part, color-keyed, graduated-grit system that can be purchased from most marble-supply houses. When I've worked through the finest grit, I rub a little marble polish on the bullnose as a final step.

Smaller Tiles Conform to the Slope of the Shower Floor

It's possible but not practical to use 12-in. tile on the shower floor. So again I cut full-size tiles into 4-in. squares. Using smaller tiles not only makes it easier to match the gradual pitch of the shower pan, but it also increases the number of grout joints for better traction on the slippery marble surface.

I spread my thinset on the floor with a ¼-in. notched trowel for the smaller floor tiles. Because of the slope of the shower floor and the ample size of the grout joints, I didn't need to butter the backs of the tiles with thinset. To add a little character to the floor, I used triangular tiles around the perimeter, which put the field tile on the diagonal. Because the shower floor was so large, I checked my rows of tile often with a framing square and a straightedge to keep everything straight and even (see the photo above).

A Corner Seat and Shampoo Shelf Are Built into the Shower Walls

When I was installing the backerboard for the shower seat, I extended it 1½ in. higher than the top of the framing, which was covered with the waterproof membrane. Instead of putting backerboard on top of the seat, I filled the extra 1½ in. with a bed of cement so that there would be no nails directly under the horizontal surface of the seat (see the photo on the facing page). This technique is a great way to avoid both staining and leaks down the road.

I also gave the cement a good ¼-in. pitch away from the walls so that water would run off the seat easily. Instead of tiles, I used a marble slab that I got from a marble supplier for the top of the seat. The solid piece of marble not only looks better than a course of tiles but also provides seamless waterproofing for one of the most vulnerable areas of the shower stall. The top of the shower threshold received a similar treatment.

I laid out the built-in shampoo shelf after I installed the first three courses of tile so that the shelf would land directly above

The marble for the seat goes on top of cement. The backerboard around the shower seat was left 1½ in. high, and then the resulting cavity was filled with cement, making the seat top virtually waterproof. A marble slab was used for the seat to eliminate grout joints.

a full-tile course. I cut the opening for the shelf in the backerboard with my grinder. The shelf cavity was framed with lengths of 2x4s that I stuck in with dabs of mastic. The mastic held the framing in place until I could screw through the board to attach the framing permanently. As I did with the seat, I pitched the shelf to shed water, but not enough to let the shampoo bottles slide out.

Clean Marble with a pH-Neutral Solution

After the marble was installed, I grouted the whole shower with a forest green grout. It's a good idea to test the grout on a tile scrap to make sure that it won't stain the marble. I mixed my grout the way I usually do, using plain water, and I spread the grout with a float and a stiff, damp sponge. Even though the wall tiles are a tight fit, I go over them to fill any hairline gaps that might be left. The grout joints between the marble floor tiles are filled the same as for ceramic tile.

I give grout a couple of days to cure before I clean the tile. Marble is sensitive to acid, so it must be cleaned with a pH-neutral cleaning solution. There are several marble cleaners on the market, and they're available at most tile stores. Avoid acidic cleaners such as vinegar, which can etch the surface of the tile and strip it of its finish. I give the marble a final rinse with clean water even after using a cleaner made for marble.

Most marble in a heavily used shower will require maintenance. Lighter marble is particularly vulnerable to staining, but all marble needs to be kept properly sealed. Two weeks after the installation, I seal the marble with an impregnator/sealer called Stand Off® Limestone & Marble Protector made by PROSOCO (see "Sources" at right). This product seals the microscopic pores of the stone. It doesn't change the appearance of the marble, but it helps repel water and prevent deep staining.

I always test the sealer on a scrap of whatever marble I've used in a project. It's best to leave it overnight to make sure there are no adverse chemical reactions on the surface of the marble.

Finally, I go over the shower walls with marble polish, which offers additional protection from soap and shampoo and gives the marble a nice, even finish.

Tom Meehan is a second-generation tile installer who has been installing tile for more than 35 years. Tom lives with his wife, Lane, and their four sons in Harwich, Massachusetts, where they own Cape Cod Tileworks.

Sources

Laticrete International Inc.
800-243-4788
www.laticrete.com
Laticrete 333 Super Flexible Additive

MAPEI
800-426-2734
www.mapei.us
Keralastic

PROSOCO
800-255-4255
www.prosoco.com
Stand Off

TEC
800-TEC-9002
www.tecspecialty.com
Super Flex

USG
800-874-4968
www.usg.com
Durock

Glass-Block Shower on a Curve

■ BY TOM MEEHAN

It wasn't long ago that shower stalls were made to serve one purpose: getting you clean. Color choice was the only real aesthetic concern; size and shape were considered matters of utility and efficiency.

Now, people think of showering as an important part of the day, both physically and mentally. The small dungeons of the past are being replaced with functional works of art. To this end, I think that glass block blows away most other shower options.

Glass-block showers are a great way to let in some light and to provide a sense of openness and freedom, even in a small bathroom. Glass blocks offer tremendous design flexibility, yet the subtle visual distortion of glass affords full privacy. No more dungeons.

New Accessories Make for an Easier Installation

If you wanted a glass-block shower a decade ago, I would have told you to find a mason—and for good reason. Unless you have experience, glass blocks are hard to keep straight and plumb. The best that beginners could hope to accomplish was a couple of courses at a time, and they would likely still struggle to keep the work in line until the mortar set up.

With just one change in design from a basic wall supported on all four sides—whether it's the addition of a curved surface, a wall that stops short of the ceiling, or one that is unsupported on one end—the project becomes more complicated. Some projects, such as the shower that's featured here, combine all these complications and then some.

Now, though, glass-block manufacturers like Pittsburgh Corning (see "Sources" on p. 44) are taking a bit of the fear out of the process by offering helpful installation accessories. The cornerstone of these accessories is the glass-block spacer. These pieces of plastic lock each block in place as it is installed, and are left in place and covered by grout. More work can be done at one time, and the blocks don't shift or slip out of place as easily.

Don't get me wrong: Glass-block installations still take patience and careful attention to detail. But I hope these installation accessories combined with my hard-learned installation tricks will help to ease what was once a much-steeper learning curve.

Build the Curb with Concrete Blocks

A straight shower curb can be built by doubling up 2x4s and nailing them to the floor, but curves are more work. For curves, I arrange a row of glass blocks on the floor into the desired shape, trace around them, cut

A curved foundation. Landscape blocks are used to create a curved foundation.

Waterproofed and pitched for drainage. The author uses a waterproof membrane and slightly pitches the marble cap to achieve proper drainage.

Cut the curves. The author uses a Gemini Revolution tile saw to cut the pieces for the top of the curb.

Preformed Kerdi corners and waterproofing strip

Establish the layout. The glass blocks are first laid dry and then traced with a pencil.

Prep the curb to hold the blocks. The marble cap is scarified in preparation for the thinset.

concrete landscape blocks to fit the shape, and set them in thinset. Next, I float a mortar bed for the shower floor.

Once the concrete blocks and mortar bed have set up, the curb is waterproofed. I like to wrap the curb in preparation for the 2-in. tiles used to cover the sides and the marble

caps that go on top. Square shower pans can be waterproofed with a one-piece vinyl membrane like Chloraloy®, but I like the Schlüter®-Kerdi system (see "Sources" for both products on p. 44; bottom photo on p. 39) for curved pans because the membrane can be cut into wedges and overlapped

Mix the Mortar Stiff

Glass blocks must be installed using a special glass-block mortar; don't be tempted to use any other products in a pinch. The lime in this powdered mortar mix is hazardous to your health if inhaled, so wear a respirator. I start with a 50-lb. bag of glass-block mortar in a small plastic mortar tub, then I slowly add water as I work the mortar with a small mixing hoe. The mortar should be fairly stiff; too loose, and the blocks will slide. To be on the safe side, I like to get the mortar close to the right consistency, then dribble a little water at a time into the tub using a grouting sponge.

The curb is coated with thinset, then the blocks are set in a thick bed of glass-block mortar.

Keep the first course sturdy and level. This first course is crucial, and each block is checked for level.

Lock it up. Glass-block spacers lock the blocks in place and keep the grout joint consistent.

where needed to get around tight curves. Because the Kerdi membrane is easily damaged, I don't set it on the shower floor until I'm done installing the glass blocks.

Before tiling the concrete-block curb, I set the waterproofing membrane for the curb in a layer of thinset. Because the curb will be visible, I cap it with marble pitched slightly toward the inside of the shower for proper drainage (see the middle photo on p. 39). To help get the marble overhang right, I tile the sides of the curb before capping it.

I cut the curved cap pieces on a Gemini Revolution tile saw (see "Sources" on p. 44) because its 10-in.-dia. ring-shaped diamond blade allows me to follow a tighter inside or outside curve than I could cut with a standard wet saw (see the bottom photo on p. 39). A standard wet saw can also be used, but you have to make a series of straight cuts up to the curved line, then remove the waste with tile nippers.

After the marble cap has been installed and has set up for a day, I dry-lay the glass blocks in place to make sure they line up properly (see the top left photo on the facing page). Once I'm happy with the layout, I trace the outline of the blocks with a pencil. Don't use a permanent marker here because the marks

Be aware. Both the straight run glass-block spacers (left) and those for curves (right) look very similar.

Panel anchors tie the glass blocks to the wall.

Expansion strips are used where the blocks meet a wall, ceiling, or header.

Joint reinforcement is used at the same horizontal joint as panel anchors.

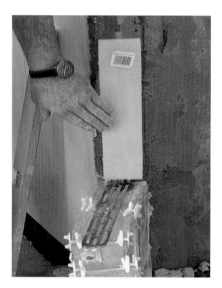

could be visible once the glass is installed. After the layout is traced onto the marble cap, I scarify the cap with a diamond blade in an angle grinder (see the top right photo on p. 40). This allows the thinset to lock into the surface of the marble cap.

Take Extra Time to Set the First Course

The first course of glass blocks sets the stage for the entire installation. Take as much time as necessary to get the blocks strongly adhered and perfectly level in both directions before moving on.

I skim-coat the curb with thinset, then set the first course of blocks on a thick bed of glass-block mortar (see the top left photo on p. 41). The thinset and mortar lock together as they dry. Check each block for level (see the top right photo on p. 41), and shim with tile spacers where necessary. It's better to use too much mortar and have it squeeze out than to use too little and risk voids.

Use glass-block spacers. They establish a consistent ¼-in. grout joint and lock the blocks in place. There are two different spacers for this project. One is for straight runs; the other is for curves (see the bottom left photos on p. 41). Be careful, though. Both spacers look similar, and they are easy to install upside down accidentally.

Reinforce as You Rise

For this job, I had an entry opening on one end of the shower wall, and the glass blocks also stopped short of the ceiling. Without using the manufacturer's panel anchors, rebar, and block spacers, the wall would have been pretty shaky. Take the time to reinforce the wall where recommended.

Sixteen-inch-long stainless-steel panel anchors tie the glass blocks to the walls (see the top photo at left). The anchors must be bent into an L-shape. The short leg should be about 4 in. long and installed every two courses.

A Pair of Levels Keeps Things in Line

Glass blocks around door openings often shift during assembly. To keep things in line, I clamp a long level to the face of the glass blocks, then clamp a short level to the long level so that I can check for plumb in two directions as I work. As new blocks are placed, I fasten them to the levels with painter's tape to keep them from shifting.

Twist off the tabs and clean. The tabs can be taken off after the blocks have set up but before the cement cures.

Always use sanded grout for large joints. It is the strongest choice.

Sources

Gemini Saw Company
310-891-0288
www.geminisaw.com
Revolution tile saw

Noble Company
800-878-5788
www.noblecompany.com
Chloraloy

Pittsburgh Corning
800-624-2120
www.pittsburghcorning.com

Schlüter Company
800-472-4588
www.schluter.com
Kerdi system

Wherever glass blocks will abut a wall, a ceiling, or a header, a ¼-in. poly expansion strip must be installed (see the center photo on p. 42). Lap the strip over the stainless-steel panel anchor. There's no need for expansion strips under the first course.

I place panel-reinforcement strips in a bed of glass-block mortar at the same horizontal joints that require panel anchors (see the bottom photo on p. 42). For curved walls, I cut the strips in half, bend them to the desired radius, and lay the halves side by side.

Clean, Grout, and Clean Again

The final stages of a glass-block installation are always the most gratifying. Remove excess mortar, pack the joints with grout, and clean the glass to a glistening shine.

The spacer tabs can be taken off after the blocks have set up a bit, usually about two to three hours (see the top left photo above). Don't wait until the cement cures, though. The excess mortar behind the tabs must be cleaned off before it hardens completely.

The strongest choice for finishing large joints is sanded grout. Pack the grout into the joints, and scrape off the excess before wiping the entire surface with a sponge and

Remove the haze. Firmly buff the blocks with a cotton cloth.

cool, clean water. After the grout has firmed up a bit, remove the grout haze by firmly buffing the blocks with a cotton cloth.

Tom Meehan is a second-generation tile installer who has been installing tile for more than 35 years. Tom lives with his wife, Lane, and their four sons in Harwich, Massachusetts, where they own Cape Cod Tileworks.

Tiling a Bathroom Floor

■ BY DENNIS HOURANY

If anything can beat ceramic tile for a bathroom floor, I'd like to know what it is. Durable and nearly impervious to water damage, tile also is adaptable to just about any architectural style. The ceramic-tile industry now offers an incredible variety of tile as well as reliable materials for setting it. If tile is more expensive than some other floor coverings, keep in mind that it can last as long as the house with little upkeep.

True enough, but a tile floor can be a nightmare if it is not laid out and installed carefully on a well-prepared subfloor. One of the key early considerations is the substrate on which the tile will be installed. Floating a mortar bed at least 1¼ in. thick used to be the

Set Full Tiles Where They Are Most Visible

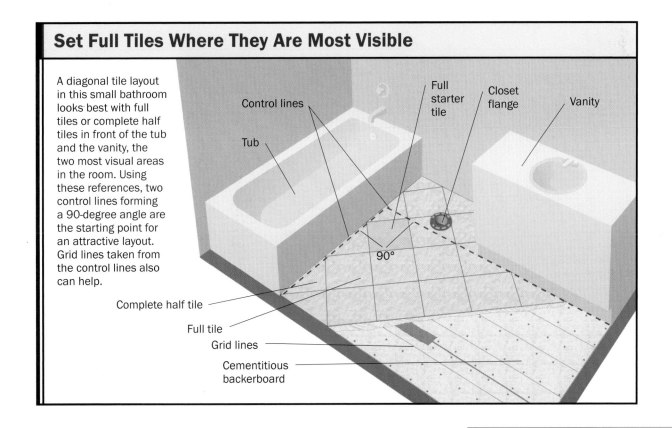

A diagonal tile layout in this small bathroom looks best with full tiles or complete half tiles in front of the tub and the vanity, the two most visual areas in the room. Using these references, two control lines forming a 90-degree angle are the starting point for an attractive layout. Grid lines taken from the control lines also can help.

Control lines

Tub

Full starter tile

Closet flange

Vanity

90°

Complete half tile

Full tile

Grid lines

Cementitious backerboard

only choice, but now there's a better option: quick-to-install cementitious backerboard.

As for the tile itself, durability and smoothness are of major concern. Most tile manufacturers rate their tiles for durability by classifying them as residential, commercial, light industrial, or industrial. For a bathroom at home, the residential grade is just fine. Smoothness is rated on a numerical scale measuring the coefficient of friction, or COF. Even though the roughness scale goes all the way to 9, I've found that a rating of 0.6 provides good slip resistance. Just keep in mind, though, that the COF goes down when the tile is wet. If you don't find the COF specified on the tile box, you can call the manufacturer for the information.

Is the floor stiff enough? A dial indicator attached to a length of iron pipe is one way to check whether there is too much deflection in the subfloor. A bouncy subfloor will result in cracked tile or grout.

Make Sure the Subfloor Is Flat

Setting tile on an inadequate subfloor is begging for trouble. The subfloor should meet deflection criteria set by the Tile Council of America (see "Sources" on p. 53)—in other words, it can't have too much bounce. If it does, chances are good that the tile will lose its bond with the backerboard or that the grout joints between the tiles will crack at the very least. The Tile Council allows a maximum deflection of ⅟₃₆₀ of the span, or the span in inches divided by 360. For example, if you have a span of 48 in., the

---

Deflection for the Non-Engineer

While the Tile Council's L-360 rule is the preferred way to determine acceptable deflection (as discussed above), it is not much help to the everyday installer. Unless you're an engineer, the rule is too difficult to apply on site. Instead, I've put together a few helpful tips. These methods are not a substitute for L-360 but they will help you avoid installation problems.

First, the obvious: Jump on the floor and have someone watch to see if there is movement or shaking. Next, and this is very important, check out the joists in the cellar, if possible. Make sure the joists are at least 2x10s without any long runs of more than 16 ft. without support. If the floor joists are 2x8s or less . . . install carpet.

Also, keep in mind that sometimes inadequate plywood or substrate might be the problem. When tiling over plywood, make sure you have a total of at least 1⅛ in. subfloor and underlayment. If you are using Schlüter-Ditra® Mat, or something equivalent, you can install the stress-crack membrane directly over a ¾-in. tongue-and-groove subfloor. In addition, using the best installation materials will make a big difference.

The bottom line is that the floor has to be structurally sound with no movement if it is going to be tiled.

Tom Meehan is a second-generation tile installer who has been installing tile for more than 35 years. Tom lives with his wife, Lane, and their four sons in Harwich, Massachusetts, where they own Cape Cod Tileworks.

most sag the subfloor can show under a load is 0.13 in., or roughly ⅛ in. Although the Tile Council calls for a minimum ⅝-in. exterior-grade plywood subfloor, houses where I've set tile often have subfloors of ⅝-in. oriented strand board, and I haven't had any problems. Minimum joist spacing is 16 in. on center (o.c.).

I can sense whether there's too much bounce simply by walking around on a floor. That's after setting hundreds of tile floors. When I started, though, I measured the deflection with a length of iron pipe and a dial indicator just to make sure (see the photo on the facing page). If there's too much deflection, don't go any further without fixing the problem.

The subfloor also must be flat. Here, the maximum amount of leeway is ⅛ in. in 10 ft. That means if you were to lay a straightedge on the subfloor, you should not be able to see a hump or a dip that exceeds ⅛ in. A wavy floor can be corrected. One way is to use a leveling compound over the wood subfloor before the backerboard is installed. You can also put the backerboard down first and then use a leveling compound that bonds to it.

In either case, the application is the same. Using a straightedge, pull some leveling compound across the low spots to fill them in. You may need to use more than one application. Leveling compounds are typically available from tile suppliers.

When Installing Backerboard, Don't Forget to Leave an Expansion Gap

Cementitious backerboard is made by several manufacturers and is readily available. I use ¼-in. HardieBacker (see "Sources" on p. 53). Sheets come in several sizes. I like this product a lot more than the backerboard with fiberglass mesh on each side. Hardie-Backer cuts cleanly and easily (see the top

The author uses Hardie-Backer, a ¼-in. cementitious backerboard, as a tile substrate. Scored on one side with a carbide tool, the board will snap cleanly with no back cut.

Glue for the backerboard. The author uses a type I mastic to bond the backerboard to the oriented-strand-board subfloor. An acrylic-modified thinset mortar also could be used.

Nail it down. Galvanized roofing nails 1¼ in. long should be driven 6 in. o.c. to install the backerboard. Set the nail heads flush with the surface.

A wet saw works best. A tile saw is the most versatile tool for cutting tile. Curved cuts start with a series of straight cuts to the layout line.

Cut crucial tile while the floor is dry. Before applying thinset to the backerboard, the author lays out the floor and cuts tiles to go around obstructions, such as this closet flange.

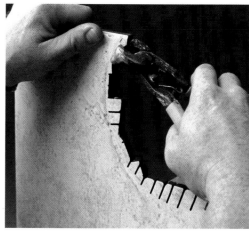

Nippers finish the job. After the author makes a rough curved cut with a wet saw, he removes the waste with tile nippers.

photo on p. 47), and it's simple to fasten to the subfloor. The ¼-in. thickness makes it easy to keep the tile at the right height, without framing a recess into the floor or having an awkward lip where the tile meets another floor surface. However, if you need to raise the level of the floor to meet an adjoining surface, you could use ½-in. cement board.

I cut and lay out the entire floor's backerboard before nailing any down. When it's laid out, joints should be staggered and edges should overlap subfloor joints. It is imperative that you leave a ⅛-in. expansion gap between sheets and a ¼-in. gap at perimeter walls or other restraining surfaces, such as cabinets.

Most manufacturers require that the backerboard be bonded to the subfloor with an adhesive, and I use type I mastic. You can use thinset adhesive, but the mastic works just as well in this application, and it's faster and easier to apply (check with the backerboard manufacturer before deciding what to use). Whatever the adhesive, put it down evenly with the notched trowel recommended by the manufacturer, and don't apply any more adhesive than can be covered with backerboard before it skins over (see the middle photo on p. 47).

I also use 1¼-in. galvanized roofing nails driven into the backerboard every 6 in. (see the bottom photo on p. 47). Nail heads should be flush with the backerboard, and if the floor is anything but tiny, you'll find a pneumatic nailer is a big help. I don't use screws because HardieBacker does not require them and they're much slower to install.

Set Control Lines for Laying the Tile, and Cut the Odd Ducks

When beginning a layout, I start by checking that walls are square and parallel. If you find things are seriously out of whack and will cause many small tiles or unsightly cuts, you may consider installing the tile on a diagonal. That's what I did here, although the reason was to add a little interest to the floor, not because the room was out of square. Diagonal layouts also have the effect of making a narrow room appear wider.

Most every room has obvious focal points where full tiles should go. I establish two control lines, 90 degrees to each other, and orient them so that they correspond with the room's focal points. For example, in the small bathroom I'm tiling here, the two critical points are in front of the vanity and in front of the bathtub; I plan on using full tiles (or complete half tiles) in these areas (see the drawing on p. 45). The cut tiles will go where they are less obvious. In general, I try to avoid cutting tiles to less than half their original size—they just look unsightly.

After you've determined the basic layout and the control lines, you can snap grid lines that will guide you as you set the tile. Plastic spacers will keep your grout lines a consistent width. But don't count on them entirely to keep the layout straight because tiles vary somewhat in size. Follow the layout lines, no matter what, for straight grout lines.

I think it's a good idea to cut some tile in advance while the floor is still free of adhesive. I don't cut all of them, just those around the closet flange or other oddly shaped spaces (see the left photo on the facing page). Once you get to a point where full field tiles (or cut tiles of a uniform size) will be used, cutting and fitting them in advance isn't necessary.

To cut tile, I use a tile saw and a pair of nippers (see the right photos on the facing page). You could use a tile board, which works by scoring and snapping tile much as you would cut a piece of glass (these tools also are called snap cutters). One disadvantage of a tile board, though, is that it can't cut L and U shapes. You can use a grinder with a diamond blade or a jigsaw with a Carborundum™ blade to cut tile. However, it's more difficult, and the cuts are not as clean.

You can't go any further without mixing up a batch of thinset mortar, which is used to bridge the seams in the backerboard and to glue down the tile. I use acrylic-modified thinset no matter what the substrate. It provides a better bond, offers more flexibility, and stays usable in the bucket longer than others. Some kinds of tile require different thinset additives, so be sure to consult with your supplier to make sure that you have the right kind.

Preparing Thinset Requires Precision

When mixing thinset, follow the directions on the bag to the letter. One requirement is that the mixture slake, or rest, in the bucket for 15 minutes after the initial mix. Then mix it again before use. Occasional stirring may help keep the thinset workable, but don't add any more acrylic admix or water much after the second mixing. I use a ½-in. drill to turn a mixing paddle between 300 rpm and 400 rpm (see the photo below).

Taping the joints between pieces of backerboard helps prevent cracks later. I use 2-in.-wide fiberglass mesh, bedding it in a layer of thinset (see the top left photo on p. 50). Make sure that the seams between sheets are completely filled. After you apply the first layer of adhesive and tape,

Stir the thinset with a slow-speed paddle. A mixing paddle turning between 300 rpm and 400 rpm does a good job of stirring up a batch of thinset. It needs to be allowed to slake, or rest, for 15 minutes before it can be used to lay tile.

Tape seams now to avoid cracks later. Fiberglass-mesh tape bedded in a thin layer of thinset spans the gap between adjoining sheets of backerboard. Skipping the tape can cause cracks to develop later.

Bed the tile in thinset mortar. When you're setting tile, plastic spacers will keep grout joints uniform in width, but following control lines is a better guarantee that grout lines will be straight.

Apply an even layer of thinset. The author uses a notched trowel to spread acrylic-modified thinset for the tile, taking care not to obscure layout lines.

Check the thinset. After setting a few tiles, lift one up to make sure they have enough thinset. Large tiles such as this one may need to be back buttered to get full coverage.

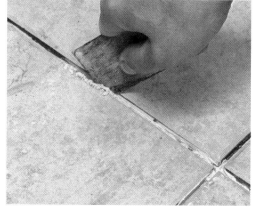

Clean out the excess thinset. A margin trowel is a perfect tool for removing thinset that has oozed into the grout joint. If grout doesn't get all the way into the joint, the resulting bond will be weak.

Does a Tile Look Off? Take It Out and Reset It

A day after setting the tile in this bathroom floor, I returned to apply the grout—and staring me right in the face was the corner of one tile that had sunk below its neighbors. Although the toilet would have camouflaged the problem, it was better to fix it before going any further.

Pulling a tile is not a big deal, providing you get to it before the thinset adhesive has had a chance to cure fully. In this case, the acrylic-modified thinset had been applied the previous afternoon, and it was still green. Using a hammer and a steel bar, I was able to jar the tile loose without too much trouble and without breaking the tile.

After scraping the semicured thinset off the back of the tile and the floor, I applied fresh thinset to both surfaces and rebedded the tile. This time, I was careful to keep the tile flush with those around it. This repair didn't take more than a few minutes, and as soon as the tile was reset, I grouted the entire floor. You never would have known anything was amiss.

you'll need to put down another layer of thinset over the tape with the flat side of a margin trowel, holding it at a 45-degree angle and pressing the tape firmly into the thinset. If you tile the floor in the same day, you can tape as you go so that you won't walk or kneel in wet adhesive. But if you wait overnight, make sure not to leave any lumps of thinset at the seams.

When applying the thinset to the backerboard for the tile, use the notched side and hold the trowel at 45 degrees to the floor so that an even amount of adhesive is applied and no air is trapped (see the bottom left photo on the facing page). What you want is 100 percent coverage of both the backerboard and the back of the tile, with about

$3/32$ in. of thinset between the two surfaces. Large tiles may have uneven backs, which will require you to back butter the surface with the flat side of a trowel.

Place the tile on the thinset with a slight twisting movement to help embed the tile fully (see the top right photo on the facing page). It's also a good idea to pull a tile off the floor near the start of the job to make sure you're using enough thinset. If the back of the tile is not fully covered, you'll know to adjust your technique or trowel or both (see the center photo on the facing page), assuming the thinset has been mixed properly. Look on the label of the thinset bag for the proper notch size.

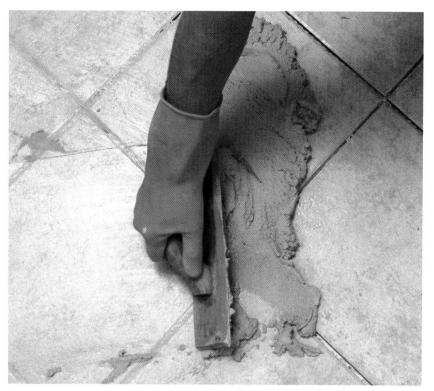

Grout mix should be stiff. Holding a grout trowel at a 45-degree angle, the author works a stiff grout mix into joints between tiles. Excess grout should be troweled off as you go.

If, after a while, the thinset becomes too stiff or if tile doesn't readily stick to it, throw it away and mix a fresh batch. Before the thinset dries completely, you should clean the excess from the joints (see the bottom right photo on p. 50). If you don't, the grout may be too thin or will hydrate unevenly—two conditions that make a weak grout line.

For a High-Strength Job, Don't Overwater the Grout

Grouting can make or break the tile job. A common mistake is adding too much water or admix when mixing the grout, which causes discoloration and a weaker mix. Another is using too much water when cleaning excess grout off the tile, which also

When a film appears, start cleaning. Not long after grout has been applied, a hazy film appears on the tile. That's a signal to start wiping the floor with a clean, damp sponge. Keep the pressure light.

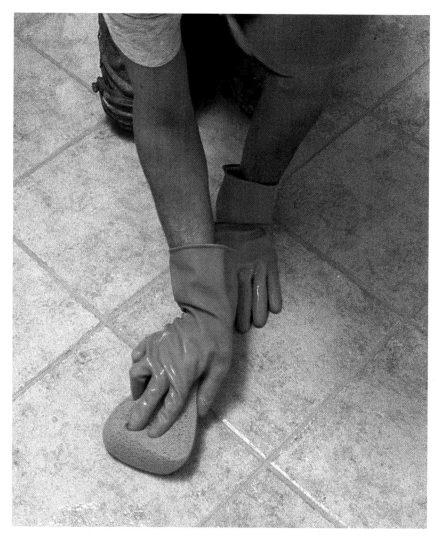

Sources

The Tile Council of America
864-646-8453
www.tileusa.com

James Hardie
888-JHARDIE
www.jameshardie.com
HardieBacker

This sponge needs a dunk. After a single light pass across the floor, this sponge has picked up plenty of excess grout. The author flips the sponge over, makes another light pass and then rinses out the sponge.

can cause it to discolor. A third common error is using a high-speed mixer for the grout, which traps air in it and makes it weak.

Add only enough water to the grout powder to make it workable. Follow the manufacturer's recommended ratio of water to grout. Ideally, the grout should be a little difficult to spread into the joints. If you're not going to mix the grout by hand, use a mixing paddle (the same type you would use for mixing thinset) and a slow-speed drill. After mixing, allow the grout to slake for 15 minutes and then remix it. At this point, you may add liquid or powder to adjust the consistency. As you work, remixing the grout occasionally will help keep it workable, but do not add more liquid.

Use a rubber grout trowel to spread the grout diagonally, holding the trowel at a 45-degree angle (see the top photo on the facing page). It's worth buying a grout trowel even if you use it only once.

With all the joints filled and excess grout removed with the trowel, let the grout sit until it begins to firm and you see a dry film on the tile. Then it's time to begin cleaning the tile. You'll need at least two good hydro sponges (sold at tile-supply stores) and a large bucket of clean, cool water. After wetting and wringing out the sponge, wipe the surface to get even grout joints. Then, with a rinsed sponge, use one side of the sponge for one wipe in a diagonal direction (see the bottom photo on the facing page). After using both sides of the sponge, rinse it out (see the photo above). Change the water frequently to avoid spreading dirty water on the tile. You may have to make several passes to remove all of the residue.

After the floor dries, you will see a film on the tile surface. This film can be polished off, but wait a bit until the grout is firmly set.

Dennis Hourany owns Elite Tile in Walnut Creek, California.

A Sloping Floor for a Barrier-Free Bath

■ BY TOM MEEHAN

One aspect of civilization that the Romans got right was the tiled bath. Since then, Europeans have built tiled bathrooms that present no distinction between the shower and the rest of the room. This design's success depends on lots of tile and a mortar substrate that slopes to a strategically placed floor drain. A lack of thresholds also makes this kind of bathroom perfect for wheelchair access.

On this side of the pond, so-called Euro-baths have found their way into the mainstream of American bathroom design, even when accessibility is not a factor. I recently completed such a bathroom for a homeowner who needed an accessible, elegant design (see the photo on the facing page).

Reframing the Floor Around the Drain Gets You Ahead of the Game

The key to a successful Euro-bath is pitching the floor to a single drain in or near the shower area. The best way to create this pitched floor is with a full mortar bed, also called a mud job. The process is similar to what is done for a shower-stall floor, only now the mud job covers the entire room.

Before taking on a bathroom of this type, I check the existing floor for level. A floor pitched strongly away from the drain is usually enough for me to pass on the job. I also make sure the floor is good and strong without any bounce.

Showers without borders. Tumbled slate, custom accent tiles, and a built-in shower seat add up to a stylish open bath that's also wheelchair-accessible.

A Contour Map Identifies Flat and Sloping Sections

With an open plan and more than 100 sq. ft. of floor area, this bathroom can accommodate both level and sloping sections of floor. Located well away from the shower, the tub and the toilet can sit on level floors. The contour lines show how the mud layer slopes to the shower drain. The pitch is about ¼ in. per ft. in perimeter areas and slightly steeper in the shower area. A slight downward slope near the doorway drops the transition height to equal the adjacent floor while letting the rest of the bathroom drain to the shower.

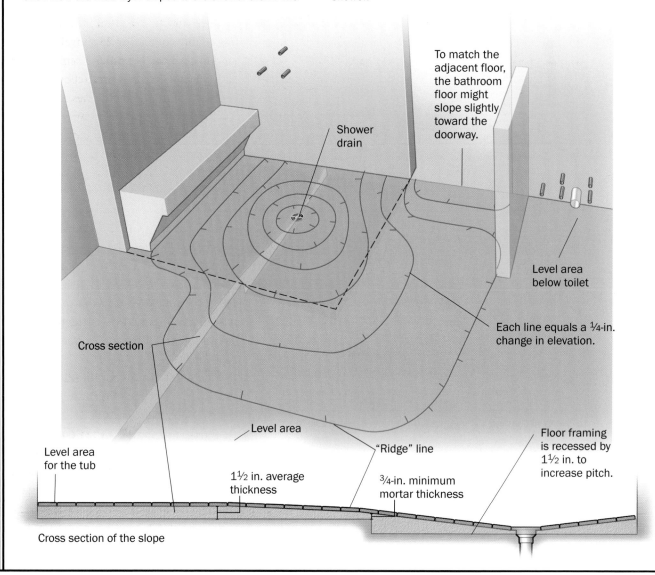

Shower drain

To match the adjacent floor, the bathroom floor might slope slightly toward the doorway.

Level area below toilet

Each line equals a ¼-in. change in elevation.

Cross section

Floor framing is recessed by 1½ in. to increase pitch.

Level area

"Ridge" line

Level area for the tub

1½ in. average thickness

¾-in. minimum mortar thickness

Cross section of the slope

To keep the finished floor from ending too high at doorways, I had the carpenters on this job frame a 1½-in. recess in the shower area, replacing the 2x10 joists with narrower 2x6s that then were tripled for added strength. When reframing isn't a viable option (on an upper floor or a slab, for instance), I get the drain as low as I can and use a smoother tile (2x2 or less) that won't impede the flow toward the drain. I also have the option of using NobleFlex® drain flashing (see the sidebar on p. 61). When the reframing was complete, I put a layer of #15 felt paper over the entire floor, then nailed down 2½-lb. diamond-mesh galvanized-wire lath with 1½-in. roofing nails, overlapping the mesh joints by at least an inch. Felt paper isolates the mortar bed from movement in the subfloor

Get a Head Start on the Slope

To increase the floor's pitch toward the drain over a short distance, the floor framing is recessed by 1½ in.

Narrower joists are tripled for extra strength.

A layer of #15 felt paper creates a barrier so that the moisture won't seep out of the mortar. To give the mortar purchase on the floor, I nail a layer of 2½-lb. diamond-mesh galvanized-wire lath over the paper with galvanized roofing nails. The mesh seams should overlap about 1 in.

and keeps the wooden subfloor from sucking moisture out of the mortar as it dries. The wire lath anchors the mortar to the floor.

Screeds Guide the Floor Pitch

In a large mortar box, I mix the mortar by thoroughly combining 25 shovelfuls of sand to each bag of portland cement; then I add water a little at a time (about 5 gal. per batch) until the mortar has a dry but stiff consistency. It should stay together when you form it into a ball in your hand. I plan for about 35 sq. ft. of coverage averaging a 1½-in. depth with each batch mixed as above.

I set the drain low enough to get a pitch of at least ¼ in. per ft. (see the drawing on the facing page). After gluing the drain flange to the PVC waste line, I dump buckets of mortar around the perimeter of the room and around the drain in 8-in.- to 10-in.-high mounds. Using a slightly wetter mortar mix, I make sure to fill the space under the flange completely.

The height of the door threshold where the bathroom floor meets the adjacent floor is the most critical juncture. Taking into account the thickness of the floor tile and the height of the adjacent floor, I pack and flatten the mortar with a steel trowel until it is the proper height. With that as a standard height, I then work my way around the room's perimeter. Because water is unlikely to reach the far corners of the room, I level the perimeter of the floor to allow the toilet, the vanity, and the tub to sit squarely.

The Shower Is a Big Shallow Bowl

Now I'm ready to pitch the floor of the shower area. I dump a few buckets of mortar between the level perimeter and the drain, and pack the mortar into that area.

So that the mortar screeds evenly, one end of the straightedge rides on the perimeter while the other end rides on the drain. As I work, I switch tools constantly, screeding with a level, packing with a steel trowel, and smoothing the surface with a wood float.

I find it easier to scrape the surface down to the finished height, so I keep the mortar slightly high, and use trowels and levels to pitch the floor to the drain. I continue to check the slant of the floor, pulling the excess mortar toward me to create a shallow bowl in the shower area.

Once the bowl is formed, the mortar is smoothed with a wood float to take out any small high or low spots. Finally, I use a steel trowel at a shallow angle to press in a tight, shiny finish.

A Membrane Waterproofs the Mud

Because mortar is porous, it needs to be waterproofed with an impervious membrane. The membrane needs not only to cover the floor but also to extend at least 6 in. up the wall.

I used Schlüter's Kerdi membrane (see "Sources" on p. 63; for this project see the sidebar on p. 61). Any nonlatex-modified thinset (also known as dry set) will attach the membrane to the mortar bed, but I used the recommended DitraSet™ (see "Sources" on p. 63).

Begin with Mounds of Mortar

A dry mix of mortar is distributed evenly around the perimeter of the room.

After cementing the drain at the proper height, I fill the space below the flange with a slightly wetter mortar mix, making sure the space is filled completely. I then distribute more mortar around the shower area.

Pack, Screed, Smooth

My basic strategy here is to bed the drain, pack the mud flat, and level around the higher perimeter of the floor, and then work at creating the slope between high and low.

I use a short level and a long aluminum straightedge to get the perimeter level.

1

2

A wooden float held at a 45-degree angle pushes the mortar tight against the wall.

3

Levels of different lengths also serve as screeds, enabling me to check the pitch of the floor while removing bumps and filling hollows.

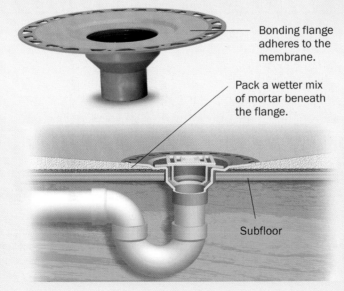

Bonding flange adheres to the membrane.

Pack a wetter mix of mortar beneath the flange.

Subfloor

4

As I pack and fair the slope of the mud, I use a wooden float to remove high spots and a steel trowel held at a low angle to finish the surface.

A Layered Membrane Seals the Mortar

To waterproof the mortar bed completely, the membrane is applied in sequence.

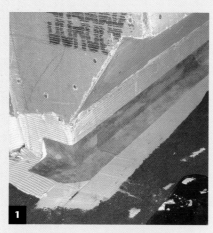

1 The inside- and outside-corner pieces are applied; any excess thin-set is squeezed out and removed.

2 A 5-in.-wide strip is folded into the seam where the floor meets the wall and is cemented in place.

After dry-fitting the first large sheet of membrane, I roll it up, then trowel thinset onto the sheet's place on the floor. A wide taping knife pushes the excess thinset to the edges and from around the drain. Successive sections should overlap by about 3 in.; I leave about ½ in. of space where the wall and floor membranes overlap the corners (see the drawing above).

3

Alternative Membrane and Drain Flashing

Many manufacturers make waterproofing membranes, but over the past 25 years, I've used two brands with great success: Schlüter and Noble (see "Sources" on p. 63 for both). Although the membranes are slightly different, they both yield the same great results. Both manufacturers also offer reliable technical support.

For this project, I used Schlüter's Kerdi membrane. The equivalent Noble product is NobleSeal® TS. I usually opt for the Kerdi because it's thinner (8 mil versus 31.5 mil for the NobleSeal TS) and therefore easier to work. Many installers choose NobleSeal TS, however, precisely because it's thicker and heavier.

Both products are covered with a thin layer of fabric on each side that lets them adhere to thinset. However, Schlüter specifies that Kerdi be installed with nonlatex-modified thinset (dry set), while Noble requires a latex-modified thinset. One major advantage to NobleSeal TS is that it acts as a crack-isolation membrane in addition to waterproofing, making it an excellent choice over substrates like wood that are likely to move over time.

NobleSeal TS comes in 5-ft.-wide rolls, while Kerdi comes in 5-in., 7¼-in., 10-in., and 39-in. widths. Kerdi makes preformed inside and outside corners; NobleSeal TS has just outside corners.

For the project featured here, I used Schlüter's drain system, Kerdi-Drain. Noble makes an interesting product called Noble Flex Drain Flashing (see the drawing at right)

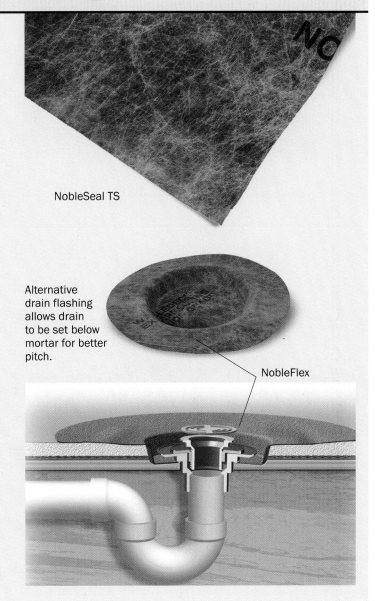

NobleSeal TS

Alternative drain flashing allows drain to be set below mortar for better pitch.

NobleFlex

that can be used with most drains that have clamping rings. Resembling an upside-down hat, this flashing fits between 16-in. on-center joists, enabling me to gain a lot of floor pitch without reframing the floor.

Tiling is the Easy Part

1

With a straightedge and a large folding square, I set the layout dry using a snapped chalkline to keep the irregular stone tile straight.

2

3

I embed a three-piece adjustable drain in thinset.

4

I use a few taps of the trowel handle to set the finished flange to the level of the tile. The rest of the floor is tiled a few rows at a time. After the tile is installed, the stone is sealed, grouted, and sealed again to complete the floor.

I begin by spreading thinset along the edges of the mortar bed and walls with a 3/16-in. V-notch trowel, then press the Kerdi preformed inside and outside corners into place. Using a taping knife with rounded corners, I squeeze out excess thinset from beneath the corners, then coat the exposed surfaces to attach the overlapping layer.

Next, I cut a length from a 5-in.-wide roll of membrane and fold it in half down the middle. Pressed into the corners, the membrane should cover each side by 2½ in. and overlap the previously installed corner pieces. As before, I flatten the membrane and squeeze out excess thinset.

Before installing the larger sections of membrane over the mortar bed, I sweep the floor thoroughly. Beginning in the shower area, I cut to length all sections and dry-fit them. The first section goes over the shower drain; I carefully mark and cut out the drain location, using a manufacturer's template.

I also use a permanent marker to draw a line onto the mortar at the edge of the first section to guide the thinset application. Each successive section overlaps the line of the previous section about 3 in. After each section is dry-fit, I roll it up, number it, and put it aside.

When all the sections are cut, I spread thinset to the first guideline with a notched trowel. Spreading the thinset in one direction, I extend it onto the flange of the drain, then slowly unroll the first membrane section, keeping the edge aligned with the guideline. As membrane is unrolled, I press it into the thinset with a taping knife, keeping the membrane straight and flat by continually pushing excess thinset to the edge of the section. After bedding each section, I spread the thinset to the overlap line of the previous section before repeating the process. Finally, I apply a floor-to-ceiling membrane to the shower walls, using the same method that I used on the floors to ensure a waterproof installation.

Smaller Tile Means Better Drainage

After the membrane sits overnight, the floor is ready for tile. I protect the membrane with felt paper or cardboard to minimize any puncture risk. The only difference from a regular tile installation is that the membrane is now the substrate for the tile.

On this job, I installed 4-in.-sq. tumbled slate on the floor. Larger tile requires a little more pitch because the tiles can't conform to the shape of the floor as well as smaller tiles. I gave this floor a little more pitch than I would for a typical handicapped-accessible bath because of the unevenness of the slate, which also can impede drainage.

I always start with a dry layout to see where the tile courses land. I try to use full tiles in areas that are seen first and most frequently. For this project, I first measured eight courses off the wall and snapped a chalkline across the room. Then I used a large folding square from C.H. Hanson (see "Sources" at right) to establish a line perpendicular to the first line. I dry-fit tiles along both lines and adjust the layout as needed. In this case, I was able to get the 4-in.-sq. drain to land perfectly within the tile layout.

With the layout set, I spread thinset and install tile the same as I would for any similar installation, working about 15 sq. ft. at a time. No matter what product is used, always follow the manufacturer's recommendations. Again, I used DitraSet to set the tile. Because the uneven surface of the tile makes it harder to clean, I gave the tile two coats of sealer before grouting and another sealer coat afterward.

Tom Meehan is a second-generation tile installer who has been installing tile for more than 35 years. Tom lives with his wife, Lane, and their four sons in Harwich, Massachusetts, where they own Cape Cod Tileworks.

Sources

Noble Company
800-878-5788
www.noblecompany.com
NobleFlex and Noble-Seal TS

Bostik
800-7BOSTIK
www.bostik-us.com
DitraSet thin-set

Schlüter Company
800-472-4588
www.schluter.com
Kerdi system and Kerdi drain

C.H. Hanson Tool Co.
800-827-3398
www.chhanson.com

Installing a Leakproof Shower Pan

■ BY TOM MEEHAN

The ultimate test. After the membrane is installed, the author plugs the drain and pours gallons of water into the shower. Better to find leaks now than after the tile is in.

In the past 10 years, I have installed well over a thousand shower pans. Of all those pans, only two have leaked. One pan belonged to my father-in-law, and the other belonged to my dentist. My father-in-law is a conservative man who likes to have all his ducks in a row. My dentist was well aware that I had two root canals coming up in the near future. Needless to say, I made sure that fixing these two jobs moved to the top of my list.

After a lot of work, I found that faulty drain-assembly fittings were responsible for the leaks in both cases (honest). In the process of rebuilding the pans, I discovered a simple test (see the photo at left) that would have saved me all that misery. But more on that later; first, let's start building the pan.

Layers of a Shower Pan

Layers of the pan alternate with drain sections and are pitched toward the drain so that water doesn't collect and rot the subfloor and framing.

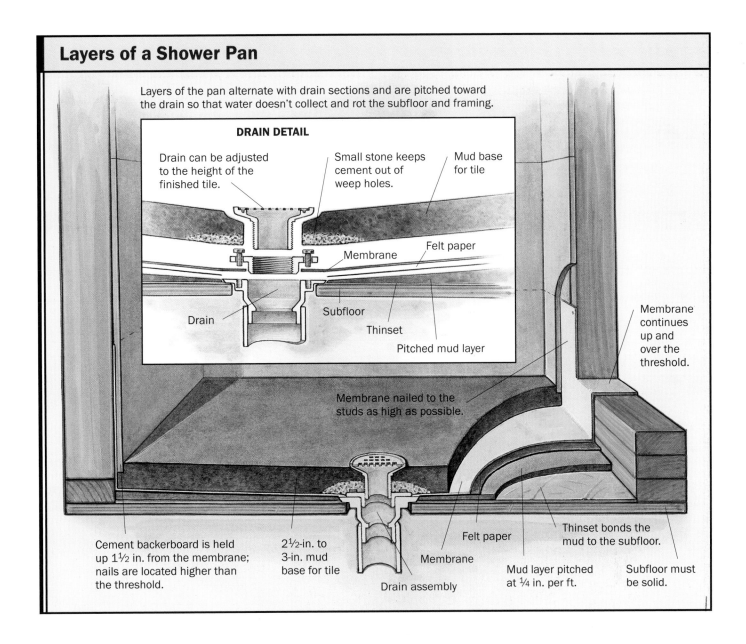

DRAIN DETAIL

Drain can be adjusted to the height of the finished tile.

Small stone keeps cement out of weep holes.

Mud base for tile

Membrane

Felt paper

Drain

Subfloor

Thinset

Pitched mud layer

Membrane continues up and over the threshold.

Membrane nailed to the studs as high as possible.

Cement backerboard is held up 1½ in. from the membrane; nails are located higher than the threshold.

2½-in. to 3-in. mud base for tile

Drain assembly

Felt paper

Membrane

Thinset bonds the mud to the subfloor.

Mud layer pitched at ¼ in. per ft.

Subfloor must be solid.

Pitch the Floor under the Membrane

Before I install the pan, I clean the subfloor in the shower area thoroughly. I look for anything that might punch or wear a hole in the membrane in the future. I set any nail heads in the lower 6 in. to 8 in. of the framing, and I put an extra flap of membrane over any nail plate installed to protect the plumbing.

When I'm building a shower pan, my first concern is that the subfloor is structurally sound. If it's not, I add a layer of ½-in.

plywood before the plumber sets the drain assembly. I also do an extra step that I think makes a huge improvement over a standard installation. I like to pitch the shower floor to the drain area before I put the membrane material down (see the drawing above). A pitched mud base allows any water that may reach the membrane to drain through the weep holes in the drain assembly.

To create this pitch, I float a layer of mud over the shower floor. The mud, a mixture of 1 part portland cement to 3 parts or 4 parts sand, is just wet enough that it holds together if you grab a handful. To bond the

Thinset begins the shower pan. After the subfloor has been swept clean, a layer of latex-modified thinset is applied to bond the layer of mud that follows.

Getting the right slant. To build up the pitch on the pan floor, a fairly dry mix of 1 part portland cement to 3 parts or 4 parts sand is used to form the mud base (above). The mix should be just wet enough to form clumps when squeezed. Using a 2-ft. level as a gauge, the author floats a pitch of about ¼ in. per ft. from the pan's perimeter to the drain (left).

Map the Membrane

The membrane is rolled out on a clean floor, and the outer perimeter of the shower pan is drawn with a felt-tip pen and labeled as fold lines. An extra 7 in. is added in each direction, and the membrane is cut to those lines (photo 1). Once the membrane is centered in the shower, the excess is carefully folded into the corners (photo 2). A roofing nail secures the fold to the framing (photo 3). As the rest of the perimeter is tacked to the studs, the membrane should not be stretched too tightly.

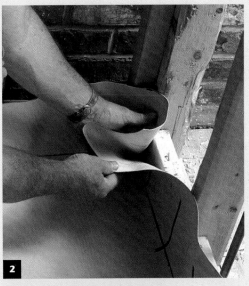

mud layer to the plywood subfloor, I first apply a layer of latex-modified thinset to the subfloor (see the top left photo on p. 66).

The mud mix is spread on top of the thinset, leaving a pitch of ¼ in. per ft. from the outside perimeter of the shower to the drain (see the top right and bottom photos on p. 66). I pack the mud with a wooden float and smooth it with a flat steel trowel. This mud layer dries overnight.

The next day, I cover the mud with a layer of 15-lb. felt paper, cutting the paper tightly around the drain. The felt paper protects the membrane from any mud grit that could abrade it. The felt paper also isolates the finished shower pan from any movement that might occur in the subfloor.

A Vinyl Membrane Keeps the Water in the Pan

Now I'm ready for the shower-pan membrane. I use a vinyl membrane called Chloraloy (see "Sources" on p. 71). I roll out the membrane on a clean floor and map out the pan with a felt-tip pen (see photo 1 on p. 67). First, I draw the four sides of the shower pan (my fold lines) and then add 7 in. to each side for the cutlines. The fold lines let me position the membrane in the shower without having to shift it around a lot. Measuring and mapping the pan also helps me avoid mistakes in my calculations. I always double-check the lines before cutting.

Folded Corners Let the Membrane Lie Flat

Before I move the membrane, I take off the top plastic ring of the drain assembly and put it aside until later. The bolts are left threaded into the lower drain assembly. I then drop the membrane into place, pushing all the fold lines to their proper outside edges.

In the corners where excess membrane bunches up, I push the liner directly into the corner with my finger. The excess corner material is then folded into a pleat so that it lies against the framing as flat as possible (see photo 2 on p. 67). Keeping the folds flat prevents bulges in the backerboard, which is applied over the membrane.

I secure the fold to the framing with one roofing nail along the top edge (see photo 3 on p. 67). As I move toward the next corner, I nail the upper edge of the liner at each stud, always keeping the liner square to the wall and taking care not to pull it off the floor or to stretch it too tight.

One of the most crucial steps is cutting and connecting the membrane to the plastic drain assembly. First, I mark the heads of the four drain-assembly bolts where they touch the membrane (see photo 1 on the facing page). Then, with a fresh blade in my utility knife, I make a small slit for each bolt and push the membrane down over the bolts. Next, I cut from bolt to bolt in a circle following the inside of the drain. Cuts should always be made toward the inside of the drain to avoid slipping with the knife and cutting the floor area of the membrane.

Because the seal between the membrane and the drain is such a crucial part of a leak-proof assembly, always lift the membrane at this point and make sure the bottom clamping ring is clear of dirt and grit. Apply the adhesive as directed by the manufacturer.

The makers of Chloraloy recommend a heavy bead of NobleSealant 150, an elastomeric caulk, between the sheet and the bottom clamping ring (see photo 2 on the facing page). Once the appropriate sealant is in place, press the bottom ring and the membrane together and then put the top ring in position (see photo 3 on the facing page). Tighten the bolts slowly, applying equal pressure on each.

At the threshold, I cut the membrane along the framed opening, fold it over, and nail it to the threshold framing. To avoid leaks at the cut corners, I fold and glue

Cut Carefully to Connect the Drain

The drain must be assembled so that it forms a watertight seal with the membrane, so membrane cuts must be precise. First, make a mark where you can feel the bolts in the drain assembly through the liner (photo 1), and cut around the bolts and the drain opening. Keep the tip of the knife pointing down and toward the plug so it won't slip. Once the liner has been trimmed, seal the space between the liner and the drain with caulk made by the same company that makes the liner (photo 2). Then put the retaining ring in place (photo 3) and tighten the bolts evenly.

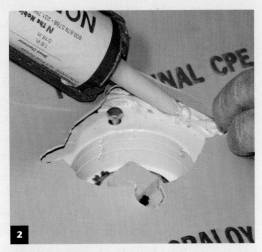

Mark the bolt locations.

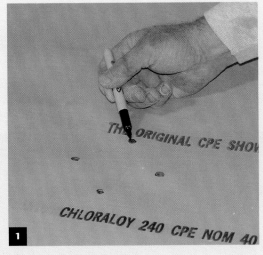

Apply the caulk.

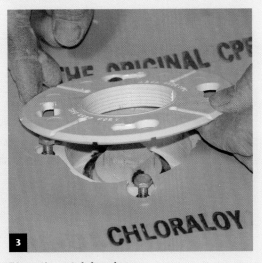

Place the retaining ring.

additional pieces of membrane into the corners with the recommended cement.

To test the pan, I first insert an expandable rubber drain plug into the lower part of the drain and tighten it with a wrench. I then dump enough water to cover the entire shower pan 2 in. to 3 in. deep (see the photo on p. 64), and I let the pan sit overnight. The next day, I make sure the level of the water hasn't gone down and then check for leaks in the ceiling directly below the shower stall.

I try to make it a point to have the builder or homeowner witness the shower-stall test.

Once the pan has passed inspection, I make sure that no one steps into the shower pan until I have poured the mud base for the tile.

Keep the Backerboard up from the Shower Floor

All the shower stalls that I tile now have cement backerboard under the wall tile. The bottom course of backerboard is installed over the membrane, but I always try to install the upper sheets and the ceiling before the pan goes in to keep big clunky feet like mine off the delicate membrane.

After the pan has been installed and tested, I put a protective layer of felt paper over the membrane while I hang the bottom pieces of backerboard. All the backerboard is attached to the studs with either 1½-in. galvanized roofing nails or galvanized screws. I make sure that the bottom pieces are at least 2 ft. wide to provide adequate strength for spanning the stud bays.

When installing the bottom course of backerboard, I keep in mind two important rules. First, I keep the board 1½ in. from the pan floor. If the backerboard is installed too low, moisture can wick up into the wall, creating a variety of problems. The second rule is never nail the board lower than the top of the threshold or the step into the shower. Nailing 4 in. from the finished floor usually works well. If the drain ever clogs, low nailing could cause a leak.

Thick Mud Makes a Sturdy Tile Base

I'm now ready to put the mud layer on top of the membrane. For this layer, I use a 4:1 mixture (sand to portland cement). I pour a couple of handfuls of ¼-in. stone around the base of the drain to help keep the weep holes in the drain assembly free and clear of cement (photo 1 below).

Pitch the Second Mud Layer Smoothly to the Drain

A couple of handfuls of pea stone (photo 1) keeps the mud mix from clogging the weep holes in the drain. The mud for the shower floor should be just wet enough to stay in a clump when squeezed in the hand (photo 2). A 2-ft. level is used to make sure that the shower floor is flat and evenly pitched to the drain (photo 3). It does, however, double as the right tool for screeding the mud. The author rounds the corners of his steel trowel so that there are no sharp corners to puncture the membrane while he's working the mud layer (see the bottom photo on the facing page).

Again, I mix the cement to a consistency that forms a ball when compressed in my hand (photo 2 on the facing page). When I'm satisfied with the mix, I dump a good amount into the pan. The weight of the mix keeps the membrane from creeping. With this shower stall, I packed the cement about 2 in. to 3 in. thick to maintain the ¼-in.-per-ft. pitch from the wall to the drain that had already been established.

I used a 2-ft. level to straighten the perimeter of the mud layer. It's a good idea for beginners to establish a level line around the pan first. Again, I use a wooden float to pack the mud. A straightedge, in this case my 2-ft. level, and a flat steel trowel let me pitch the mud smoothly and evenly to the drain (see photo 3 below). The upper portion of the

drain can be adjusted so that it will be flush with the installed tile.

One precaution I take is to round over the corners of the steel trowel (see the bottom photo below). A square corner could slice or puncture the membrane if I'm not careful. I keep working the surface to eliminate any voids or low spots in the mud that can collect water once the tile is installed. When the mud layer is smooth, evenly pitched and level around the perimeter, I let it sit overnight, and then I'm ready to install the tile in the morning.

Tom Meehan is a second-generation tile installer who has been installing tile for more than 35 years. Tom lives with his wife, Lane, and their four sons in Harwich, Massachusetts, where they own Cape Cod Tileworks.

Sources

Noble Company
800-878-5788
www.noblecompany.com
Chloraloy and Noble-Sealant 150

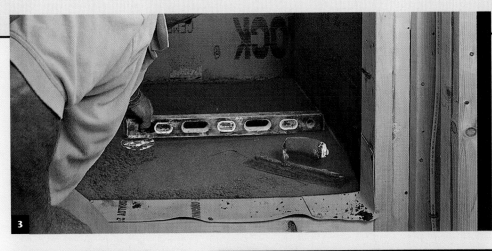

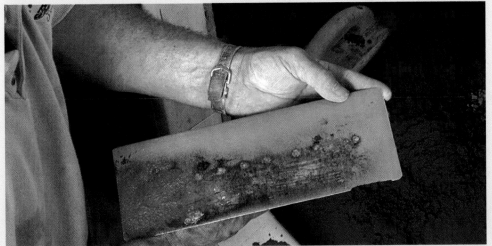

Bubble Bath

■ BY MARIA LAPIANA

When we set out to remodel a bath, most of us have only one bath in mind—at least at any given time. Not so for Nanae Nakahara, a San Francisco Bay Area interior designer who was enlisted to design three and a half baths simultaneously—as well as a kitchen—for a client in Berkeley, California. Unfazed, the Japanese-born Nakahara took on the project with equanimity, creating clean, discrete spaces, all reflecting the homeowner's contemporary tastes.

The en-suite guest bath is especially captivating. It's not a grand or spacious space, yet Nakahara designed it with spot-on sophistication and more than a dash of whimsy. Making the project particularly rewarding, says Nakahara, was that she and her client (a violin instructor who also teaches in Japan in the summer) shared the same sensibility

and appreciation of pared-down, Asian-inspired design.

Nakahara remembers, "The homeowner wanted something unique, not what everyone else has. Nothing that could be found in any house, anywhere." She was open to ideas—and the designer had plenty.

Because the bath is accessible only through the guest bedroom and isn't visible from the rest of the Craftsman-style house, Nakahara decided she had more latitude to let loose in terms of style. And because it's a guest bath, used infrequently, Nakahara didn't have many of the constraints of a typical bathroom: considerations of daily use, the required cleaning that goes along with it, and storage. "I really felt as though I had the freedom to design this bath any way at all," she says.

Common materials, creative use. Designer Nanae Nakahara and tilesetter Oded Heinrich made this small guest bath stand out by creating glass-tile "bubbles" on the shower wall and "waves" along the wainscot.

Making Waves—and Bubbles

The "bubble" pattern on the rear wall of the shower was designed by Nanae Nakahara; the installation was done by Berkeley master tilesetter Oded Heinrich. Because Heinrich says he likes to work "by demonstration," he walked through the complete process with the designer before cutting a single tile.

To start, Heinrich drew three "bubble" templates on paper (measuring 8 in., 10 in., and 12 in.) based on Nakahara's drawings. He laid the marble field tiles on the floor as they would appear on the wall, being careful to match color and grain. He then laid the templates over the tiles and consulted with Nakahara on the correct placement of the bubbles. He marked the tiles accordingly, then cut away the circles using a wet saw fitted with a diamond blade.

Because the mosaic glass tiles are mounted on mesh backing, Heinrich used a utility knife to cut the tiles into approximate circles. After installing the marble tiles, then the glass circles in the negative space, he filled in the bubble borders with single tiles as needed to complete the look.

To create the "wave" pattern atop the wainscot, Heinrich trimmed ¼-in. cement backerboard to create the shape, scratch-coated it with modified epoxy, then set the tiles. He opted not to cut any of the small glass tiles for fear of cracking them or, worse, diminishing the soft, rounded appearance of the "waves."

Heinrich says he is pleased with the payback that can be realized from the combination of creative planning and tile cutting. "We wanted to create a million-dollar look—without spending a million dollars," he says.

0 0.5 1   2ft.

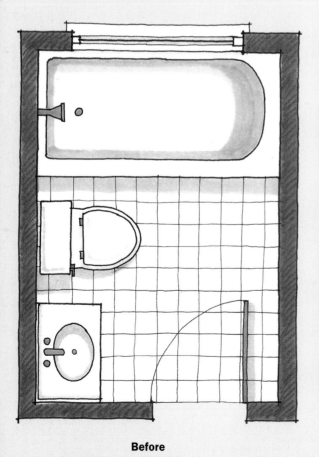

Before

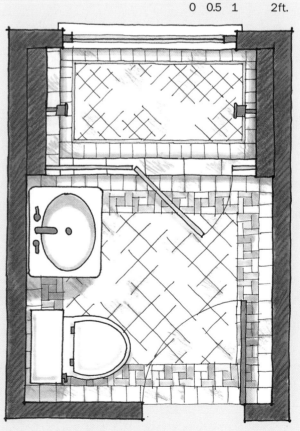

After

Creatively mixing different types of tile can create a stunning bath, but it should be done with care. Here are some tips from interior designer Nanae Nakahara.

Framed. Porcelain tiles in a pinwheel pattern frame the floor.

Double-check sizes

Sometimes the actual size of the tile you choose is different from what is advertised. For example, a "12x12" tile may in fact measure only 11¾-in. square. If sizes vary within an order, you'll need to double-check as you go.

Check grout lines, too

When using more than one type of tile, note the size and thickness of each to be sure the grout lines will meet. For example, if you combine 6-in. by 6-in. tiles with 12-in. by 12-in. tiles, grout lines should line up. If you're using smaller tiles for an accent or border, though, it's OK if lines don't match exactly.

Consider edge profiles

When using tiles that vary in thickness, be sure the thicker tiles have grazed—or finished—edges because unfinished edges are more visible. Another workaround is to have the tilesetter build up a mortar bed for thinner tiles. The bed allows thin tiles to be set flush with thicker tiles.

Tile, Four Ways

To make the small space memorable, Nakahara used four different tiles (see "Tile Tips" above), with an effervescent pattern stealing the show on the rear wall of the shower. "I wanted to create something like a fantasy, with the circular tiles appearing to be bubbles," she says. "Tiles are almost always square or rectangular. I wanted something that was not so geometric."

The room's palette was inspired by the homeowner's preference for shades of green. Green accents were used in another bath in the house, but in this room, green was chosen as the predominant color.

Nakahara selected 12-in. by 12-in. marble tiles for the walls and white glass "pebble" tiles to serve as the striking contrast material that forms the "bubbles." Cutting the marble tiles into circles and then setting the glass tiles on the wall was time-consuming, but Nakahara says she was fortunate to have worked with a patient, skilled tilesetter (see "Making Waves—and Bubbles" on p. 74).

The designer opted for 6-in. by 6-in. tumbled-marble tiles for the floor and 4-in. by 4-in. tiles in the shower. (The smaller

Be creative, but don't go overboard

It's perfectly OK to combine ceramic, porcelain, stone, glass, or metal tiles. By combining accent, chair-rail, pencil, border, and insert tiles with field tiles, you can create a wide variety of designs. There's no hard-and-fast rule, but four different tile choices are acceptable in the average 5-ft. by 8-ft. bath. Colors should be limited, too. Most important is that they harmonize with one another.

Work mosaic magic

Mosaic tiles make great accents. They can be cut into irregular shapes, and field tiles can be cut to mold around them. When using glass tiles, always use white thinset. This allows the light to shine through and the tiles to show their true colors.

The buildup. Heinrich built up the wall with ¼-in. backerboard before applying modified epoxy and glass tile to create a wavelike border over the bathroom's tile wainscoting. The fixtures were kept simple so that they wouldn't compete for attention with the tile.

Sources

DESIGNER
Nanae Nakahara, CKD CBD
650-347-6196
www.eleganceredesigned.com

LIGHTING
Hinkley
216-671-3300
www.hinkleylighting.com

PLUMBING PRODUCTS
Hansgrohe
800-334-0455
www.hansgrohe-usa.com

Kohler
800-456-4537
www.kohler.com

TILE PRODUCTS
Casa Dolce Casa
www.casadolcecasa.com

Custom Building Products
800-272-8786
www.custombuildingproducts.com

MS International
www.msistone.com

Pacilantic
407-880-3032
www.pacilantic.com

shower tiles allow a more gradual downward grade toward the drain.) Porcelain tile in a deeper hue was used to create the pinwheel border on the floor.

To complete the look, Nakahara specified more glass pebble tiles to create a wave pattern atop the wainscot wall tiles. The carefully crafted border works as a backsplash behind the sink and an eye-catching accent around the rest of the room.

Because the tilework is admittedly overpowering, Nakahara kept the rest of the room's components simple. The white Kohler fixtures are classic in style. The light

fixtures, showerheads (one fixed, one handheld), sink faucet, and hardware, including towel and grab bars, are all an understated brushed nickel.

For all her creativity, Nakahara gives credit to her client. "Designers are not like artists, who merely have to fulfill their own needs," she says. "We must work to fulfill our clients' needs…and I was very fortunate to have someone trust me in this way."

Maria LaPiana writes about home design, health, and wellness.

Bathroom-Tile Design

■ BY LYNN HOPKINS

Walk into a tile showroom, and you may be overwhelmed by the sheer number of colors, materials, finishes, and sizes available. The best way to keep your wits about you is to develop a strategy beforehand for the style of bathroom you plan to create. This plan will help to guide tile selection and installation.

Before going to the store, think about the character of your new bath. Are you interested in a traditional bathroom with historical references, something with fixtures and finishes that remind you of an earlier time? Or are you dreaming of something more sleek and modern?

Regardless of the style of bathroom you choose, designing a tile installation requires forethought. The accompanying drawings illustrate key areas to consider when developing a tile design and show how the traditional or modern character of the room might influence tile selection and layout. As part of the planning process, I recommend making detailed drawings that show which tiles go where on both the floor and the walls. An accurate, scaled sketch of a section of wall and floor, plus any special corner conditions, makes it much easier to order, lay out, and correctly install the tile.

Start by Planning the Walls

There are three standard heights to consider when tiling a bathroom wall: wainscot height, shower height, and full-wall height. You may use one, two, or all three of these heights in a single bathroom, depending on the look you are trying to achieve and on your budget. Because tiled walls are more expensive than wallboard, tile often is used only where it is needed most: on the lower portion of the wall that requires water protection. This wainscot is usually between 36 in. and 42 in. tall, enough to provide a backsplash of 4 in. or so above the sink. Tile protects the walls below towel bars from wet towels, and the walls around the toilet from the spray of rambunctious kids.

Tiling to wainscot height may be adequate protection around tubs without showers as most splashes occur below this line. In a shower area, however, all enclosure walls should be tiled high enough to protect the walls from water spray, at least 72 in. and preferably to the ceiling.

Details for a Traditional Bathroom

3-in. by 6-in. brick tiles

1-in. by 6-in. color band

Fixtures are centered on tile layout.

1 Shower enclosure is tiled to at least 72 in.

At least 4 in.

36 in. to 42 in.

Bullnose tiles

Border tiles define limits of the room.

2

6-in. by 6-in. tiles

1. TURNING CORNERS

Profiled edge tiles

2. INSIDE CORNERS

A bathroom with traditional characteristics has plumbing fixtures that take their styling cues from an earlier era, generally the 1920s or 1930s. The tile should reinforce these historical references. Small wall tiles, such as 3 in. by 6 in., 4 in. by 4 in., and even smaller mosaics, were typical in the old days, in part because the adhesive available could not support tiles that were much larger and heavier than 6 in. sq.

Traditional styles often celebrate the edges where tile meets wall or where wall meets floor with a border or fancy molding profile. Borders run around the perimeter of the floor and/or walls, defining the limits of the room.

Choose the Right Tile

Tiles finished on only the front face are called field tiles. When installed, they are butted next to each other with grout filling the spaces in between. Wherever wall tile stops short of the ceiling, field tiles should not be installed on the top row because the raw, unfinished edge of the tiles will be exposed. For these locations, use tile with at least one finished edge. Typically, the finished edge is a rounded bullnose shape that makes an elegant transition from tile to wall surface. In bathrooms with traditional styling, this transitional edge frequently is celebrated with a decorative border that intro-duces a band of color, a pattern, a texture, or a special profile (see the drawings on p. 79).

Borders Create a Transition

Although a decorative border is a great way to handle the tile-to-wall transition, you'll need to consider how to handle the border when the tile goes from a lower to a taller height. In a traditionally styled bath, I prefer to turn the edging and keep the border moving up, over, and down again, using mitered corners at each turn. I find that a miter creates a crisp, clean look and allows the flexi-

Details for a Modern Bathroom

The details in a modern room imply expansiveness and continuity. Tile frequently runs continuously from floor to ceiling or from corner to corner. Borders like those found in a traditional bath are seldom used because they would feel constrictive. Luxurious materials, such as stone, are treated simply so that nothing competes with or detracts from the beauty of the material itself.

Modern designs often use larger tiles—8 in. by 8 in., 6 in. by 12 in., 12 in. by 12 in., or 16 in. by 16 in.—because they feel more expansive. Visual interest comes from the use of multiple materials, patterns, textures, and plane changes. In this example, the height change at the shower area is emphasized with a bump-out separating the plumbing wall into two different planes. Within the shower, 12-in. by 12-in. stone tiles run floor to ceiling. The side edges of the stone tile are mitered to finish the outside corner. Outside the shower, 6-in. by 12-in. ceramic tiles are used on the walls. The running-bond pattern helps to tie the different materials together.

12-in. by 12-in. stone tiles

Running-bond pattern is an easy, inexpensive way to add visual interest.

Bump-out, 2 in. minimum

6-in. by 12-in. ceramic tiles

3

3. CHANGING PLANES

Room feels more expansive with large floor tiles.

Inside corner marks transition from large shower tiles to smaller wall tiles.

Mitered outside corner

bility to use border designs without a special corner tile (see the inset drawing on p. 79).

Other areas that demand careful planning are corner borders at wall intersections. If your bath has only inside corners, you will need tiles that are finished only on the face and one edge. Outside corners—those that project into the room—require tiles finished on the face, the top, and one side. If you use tile with a profile, you'll need a special outside-corner tile. Not all tile manufacturers or lines include these special pieces.

The baseboard area, at the junction of wall and floor, is another opportunity for a decorative border. If you used a color band at the top of the tiled wall, a second band of color would work well at the bottom. If not, consider a base tile that is taller than the wainscot tiles. You can choose base tiles with a profile that incorporates a radius to meet the floor tiles.

Floor Tiles Take a Cue From the Walls

Floor tiles need to be more durable and slip-resistant than wall tiles, so be sure to select a type intended for floor installation. The safety and durability characteristics of floor tiles may give them a different look than that of wall tiles. To tie the two surfaces together visually, use the same color, texture, pattern, or other design feature from the walls in the flooring. In a traditional bath, for instance, you might use a border of the same color on the walls and the floor.

Another strategy is a floor patterned with a mix of small and large tiles, where the color of the small tiles matches that of the wall tile. Smaller tiles result in more grout lines, which give the floor more texture and make it less slippery. The additional grout is more susceptible to dirt and mildew, however.

Center Tile Layout on Entries and Fixtures

Many tile-layout guidelines suggest positioning the layout on the center of the room and cutting the tiles around the perimeter to fit. These guidelines recommend centering the pattern on either a tile or a grout line, depending on which choice results in the largest tiles around the edges of the room. This is a good place to start, but you may want to adjust your design in response to other features in the room.

One of the typical ways your eye determines whether a pattern is centered is by comparing the end tiles: If the tiles on each end are equal in size, you assume the pattern is centered. However, if your eye cannot easily compare the end tiles to each other, you'll look for other cues, such as alignment.

Sometimes, especially in large rooms, it is preferable to center tiles along lines of sight or movement. By following this strategy, the tile pattern is centered on the person using the bathroom. Tiles centered on the entry door are centered on the person who walks through that door; wall tiles centered on the sink and on the mirror above are centered on the person looking in that mirror. Tiles centered on the showerhead and control valves also are centered on the person using the shower.

If tile has been centered on the key sink and shower walls, the layout frequently is mirrored on the opposite wall. Centering tile on the sink and the shower controls may be difficult if the sink and the shower are on the same continuous wall; but this design should be possible if the distance between the centerline of the shower or tub fittings and the sink is a multiple of the tile size.

Mark out the tile design before any rough plumbing work is done; then adjust fixture placements as required for the most attractive finished room. Alignment and centering of fixtures, tiles, and sightlines reinforces the organizing principles of the design. People subconsciously find that reinforcement reassuring and, consequently, attractive.

Lynn Hopkins (www.lhopkinsarch.com), an architect specializing in residential design, is based in Lexington, Massachusetts.

Details from Great Bathrooms

Benches, shelves, and hooks. Don't overlook the convenience of a small bench where you can sit and shave, shelves that can hold soap and shampoo, and some open wall space for towel hooks and bars.

Tile put to good use. Variations in tile size highlight architectural details, while glass-block tiles let in plenty of light.

Bold and beautiful. The play of light and color in this bathroom isn't an accident. It's what happens when an architect plans a bathroom remodel with an artist.

Accentuate the positive. Large, rectangular porcelain tiles installed vertically draw attention to the shower's high ceiling while the mosaic-tile floor provides plenty of traction.

Liven up a bland room. Blue and white mosaics splash color across the sink wall in this St. Paul, Minnesota, remodel.

Color coordination. Staying in the same color family ties together the mosaic pebble floor and the wall of sleek subway tiles.

Updating a tradition. Designed to capture the calm richness of traditional Japanese architecture but with a modern focus, this bathroom was created with wall and shower tiles by Casalgrande Padana and custom-cut slate floor tiles.

Balancing the budget. Saving on white ceramic floor and wall tile freed up money for the aqua-colored glass mosaic wall tile.

Use tile to differentiate. On the floor, a switch from 13-in. ceramic tile to 2-in. tile (by Cerim Ceramiche) distinguishes the shower from the dry part of the room. On the walls, a mosaic strip (by Cerámica Tres Estilos) adds zip.

Let loose. A child's bathroom is a great place to have fun with tile. This bathroom features a whimsical countertop of brightly colored tile.

Putting Tile to Work in the Kitchen

■ BY LANE MEEHAN

Our black Lab, Bogey, is a walking mud factory and sheds so much that he should be bald. When it came time to choose tile for our kitchen floor, we looked for tile that would help disguise evidence of Bogey and our three active boys. We chose a tile that looks like stone but in a color and finish that could hide dirt and dog hair until I had a spare moment to run the vacuum.

Our choice was based primarily on ease of maintenance, just one consideration when choosing kitchen tile. As a tile-store owner with a background in design, I field questions all the time about incorporating tile into clients' kitchens. This chapter addresses the questions I am asked most frequently.

What Types of Tile Can I Choose From?

The two most basic categories of tile are stone and ceramic. Stone tile is a natural product, mined or quarried directly from the earth. The three most common stones used

for tile are granite, marble, and limestone, with granite being the hardest.

Stone in its natural state is porous, so wherever it's used in a kitchen, it must be sealed to resist staining and discoloration. Stone tile has color all the way through, so deep scratches won't expose a different base color. However, a highly polished surface on a stone tile seems to accentuate even the smallest scratches. Stone can be installed on floors, countertops or backsplashes; however, it does tend to be a high-maintenance product.

On the other hand, ceramic tile is made from clay rolled flat and either sun-baked or fired in a kiln. There are hundreds of different clays, each with its own characteristics that can vary the tile's performance. Color is applied to ceramic tile in the form of baked-on glazes that also seal the tile.

In the past, ceramic-tile finishes had problems standing up to heavy use and abuse, but with recent technical advances, ceramic tile now performs better than it used to. With most ceramic tile, the color is

Tile outlines and defines kitchen spaces. A tile border gives the island in this kitchen, designed by Tim Quigley of Minneapolis, its own separate visual space. The backsplash behind the stove forms a functional accent.

just on the surface, so deep scratches expose the clay below.

Porcelain is another manmade tile product. Porcelain is much denser than ordinary ceramic, making it harder to scratch and break. But as with stone, the shinier the surface of ceramic or porcelain, the more scratches will show. So I try not to use high-gloss tiles anywhere in a kitchen except on backsplashes, areas that are less susceptible to scratching. In the past, porcelain has been more expensive than ceramic, but improvements in technology have reduced the price.

Beyond the amount of gloss, tile finishes can vary greatly. Tile finishes are graded by their ability to resist wear due to traffic; a light-industrial tile has a higher durability rating than most residential-grade tiles. Industrial-rated tile is a bit more expensive, but the extra cost makes sense if your kitchen resembles a freeway. In addition to a durability rating, the Tile Council of America (see "Sources" on p. 94) gives tile a coefficient of friction (COF) rating, which indicates how slippery the surface will be underfoot. But if the tile feels too smooth or too slick to the touch, it will probably be too slippery to use on the floor.

How Do Lifestyle and Lighting Affect Choices?

The first thing I ask clients about is their family, their lifestyle, and the way their kitchen is going to be used. For example, for a client who has a large family or who does a lot of entertaining, the kitchen is a busy hub with a casual atmosphere. For this kitchen, I might suggest warm-colored tile with perhaps a softer stone look.

After the client's lifestyle, I look at the type of lighting in the kitchen. If it is blessed with a great deal of natural light from windows or skylights, tumbled marble tile or tile with a matte finish will absorb light and create a softer look (see the photo on p. 90). A textured surface on the tile softens the effect even further.

On the other hand, tile with a glossy finish reflects light and helps brighten areas of a kitchen that are dimly lighted or that receive little or no natural light. Remember that glossy tile used in a kitchen with a lot of light, either natural or artificial, requires more frequent cleaning because fingerprints and water spots tend to show up more.

When choosing tile, I also look at the color and finish of the cabinets and countertops. If the counters and cabinets have a matte or satin finish, then I try to keep the same feel in the floors and the backsplash. By the same token, if the kitchen has the

Tile Offers Almost Endless Options

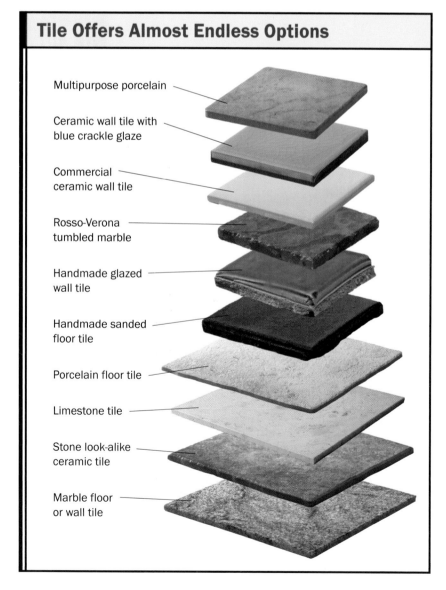

Multipurpose porcelain

Ceramic wall tile with blue crackle glaze

Commercial ceramic wall tile

Rosso-Verona tumbled marble

Handmade glazed wall tile

Handmade sanded floor tile

Porcelain floor tile

Limestone tile

Stone look-alike ceramic tile

Marble floor or wall tile

Ceramic Tile: Porcelain vs. Nonporcelain

All tiles made of clay and cured by heat are ceramic tiles. However, ceramic tile is best understood by dividing it into two product classifications: porcelain and nonporcelain. Their availability and look are roughly the same, but their durability is not. Thanks to a balance in the market, porcelain tiles can now be had at nearly the same price as nonporcelain products.

Porcelain tile is more durable

Porcelain tiles are created by mixing porcelain clay and very finely ground sand, and curing them with high heat and pressure. Porcelain tile is denser and harder than nonporcelain tile and has a lower water-absorption rate of 0.5% or less. Porcelain's density makes it highly resistant to physical damage, while its low absorption rate makes the tile frost resistant, allowing it to be used outdoors. Unglazed porcelain tile is sought after for its full-body characteristics, which means its color remains consistent throughout the tile. Surface scratches and damage are less noticeable as a result, a benefit that diminishes when the tiles are glazed. Also, when some porcelain tiles are glazed, they are no longer guaranteed to be frostproof.

Nonporcelain tile is easier to work with

Nonporcelain tiles are made primarily of clay mixed with minerals and water. The material is then fired to solidify the tiles into a bisque form. This process creates tile that isn't as hard as porcelain, so it can be worked more easily with basic snap cutters and nippers instead of a wet saw.

In most cases, a sealer and a glaze are applied to the surface of nonporcelain tile to create color and texture before the tile receives a second firing. The glaze applied to nonporcelain tile can make it extremely durable, but never as durable as porcelain.

Nonporcelain tile's main weakness is that it has a water-absorption rate of greater than 0.5%. As a result, the tile doesn't perform nearly as well as unglazed porcelain tile in outdoor freeze/thaw environments.

The top choice when strength matters most. Although nonporcelain tiles can be quite durable, none are as resilient as porcelain.

Buy what looks good. Even though damage to nonporcelain tiles is more noticeable than with some porcelain tile, they can be purchased in grades that are perfectly suited for high-contact areas like kitchen counters and floors.

Tile can act as a dimmer switch. This kitchen gets lots of light from two sides. The natural colors and matte finish of the tumbled-marble countertop and backsplash help soften the light and cut down on glare in a kitchen with a lot of windows.

polished, streamlined look of many contemporary kitchens, I suggest a straightforward tile pattern with a glossy finish.

Tile color can make a large contribution toward a warm or cool feel in a kitchen. The earthy tones of limestone or tumbled marble are the warmest of the tile colors, while bright whites and blues tend to be quite cool. But even cool colors can be warmed with colored grout. For example, an ivory or off-white grout color can take the cool edge off bright white. The reverse can be true if you're trying to achieve a formal or industrial feel with gray or blue tile. A steel-gray grout helps create a crisp, cool look.

Will My Three Boys and the Family Dog Hurt My Tile Floor?

A client's lifestyle has the biggest bearing on the choice of floor tile. If you'd rather spend time with your three growing boys than take care of your kitchen floor, I suggest tile that hides a multitude of sins (and dirt) and always seems to look nice, such as a ceramic-stone look-alike (see the photo on the facing page).

A quick vacuum and an occasional mopping, and you're off and running.

If cooking and entertaining are big parts of your life, then I'd suggest tile that won't stain if hot grease and oil or an occasional glass of wine is spilled on it. A glazed ceramic tile works best in this situation, but for an Old World look, you can use a real stone, such as limestone. If you select a stone-tile floor, be sure to treat it with a good sealer according to the manufacturer's directions. We recommend either Miracle Sealants' Porous Plus or One Master Marble and Stone Care's Gold Shield (see "Sources" on p. 94) for sealing stone tile.

No matter what tile you choose for your kitchen floor, the grout should also be sealed. To make the grout more impervious to spills and stains, I recommend starting with a latex-modified grout or one that is mixed with a latex additive instead of water. Once the grout has cured properly, a sealer such as Miracle Sealants' Porous Plus will fight off most food incursions.

Another grout option is epoxy, which is stain resistant and does not require sealing. But because epoxy is harder to work with for the installer, we generally use it for smaller

No time for cleaning? For busy, active families with kids and pets, consider a tile floor with a lot of color variations such as this stone look-alike. It stays better looking longer between cleanings.

areas, such as countertops. With some tile, such as limestone, epoxy grout is not recommended, so be sure to check with manufacturers' suggestions.

How Does a Tile Floor Relate to Adjacent Rooms?

The kitchen-floor tile should help establish a visual flow into the surrounding areas, so I ask clients about the colors and materials on the floors of the rooms that are adjoining the kitchen. For example, if the kitchen floor joins up with a dark wood floor in the dining room, consider using tile with a warm, medium color to cut down on the visual contrast between rooms. If the kitchen floor meets colored carpet in an adjacent room, keep in mind that you'll probably change the carpet at some point, so choose a neutral tile color that will go with future carpet choices.

Tile thickness is another consideration. Whether the kitchen floor butts up against other existing tile, hardwood floors, or carpet, the tile installer will need to install

some sort of threshold to create a clean transition into the next room. Tile thickness can also affect doors that swing into the kitchen, as well as appliances, such as dishwashers or trash compactors, that have to fit under the countertops in a kitchen.

Can Tile Make My Tiny Kitchen Look Bigger?

Tile layout can have a big impact on a room's appearance. While a parallel or straight pattern can intensify the narrowness of a kitchen, a diagonal tile pattern makes a room look wider (see the sidebar on p. 93).

Tile size can also affect the appearance of the room. The smaller the tile, the busier the grout–joint pattern. The simple grout–joint pattern you get with larger 10-in. to 12-in. tiles can make a small room look larger. Smaller 4-in. to 6-in. tiles on a floor can have the opposite effect, creating a mosaic pattern or a cobblestone look.

Clipping the corners of square tiles creates hexagons or octagons with small square spaces left between. The small tiles (called dots) that fill the spaces can introduce a dash of color to the floor in a pattern that breaks up the simple straight lines.

Irregular tile patterns such as block random (using three sizes of tile) or a pinwheel pattern can help unify a kitchen that has many entrances and exits. These patterns also work well to blend together tile that is highly varied in color. A tile border on the floor can make a kitchen look cozier by bringing the eye in or by creating a frame around the kitchen table or an island (see the photo on p. 87).

Is Tile OK for a Kitchen Countertop?

Granite-slab countertops have long been popular in high-end kitchens. Tile countertops, both ceramic and stone, have some of the same attributes as slabs, such as durability and heat resistance, but at less than half the cost, depending on the tile you choose.

Granite tile can be installed with tight grout joints to give the impression of a solid slab. And with granite tile, it's easy to add a border to accent or complement the color of the stone. One drawback to stone tile on a countertop is the edges. Although you can round over the edges, granite tile is thinner than a solid slab (3⁄8 in. to 1⁄2 in. compared with 1 1⁄4 in., normal thickness for a granite slab), so it's tougher to get the same full-slab look. Another drawback is not being able to install an undermount sink with granite tile.

Although the tight grout joints of granite tile create a good, smooth work surface, machine-made ceramic tile with standard grout joints makes a slightly rougher work surface.

Handmade tile is usually installed with wider grout joints that are charming, but its inherently bumpy surface can be difficult to work on and can cause wine glasses and bowls to tip over (see the photos at left).

The edges of a tile countertop can be addressed in various ways. Continuing the tile over the edge gives the countertop a thick look. Relief tile, such as a rope pattern, can turn countertop edges into a visual focal point. Wooden edges that match or complement cabinets are also popular.

As on floors, borders on countertops can add decoration. But if it's used in too large an area or if a lot of items are stored on the counter, a border can be lost or distracting.

Tile can also be combined with other types of surfaces for a dramatic look (see the photo on p. 90). For instance, the savings from tiling most of the countertop might leave enough money for a solid slab of granite in the sink area for an undermount sink. A stone slab or a wood surface on only the island could make a bold statement while providing a smooth surface for an informal eating area.

Handmade tile is pretty but uneven. The irregular surface of handmade ceramic tile is a challenge to work on and can be hazardous to wine glasses. Cutting boards should always be used on tile countertops.

Tile Patterns at Work

The right pattern can make a kitchen look wider. Floor tile installed in a straight pattern makes a narrow room seem narrower (see the left photo below) while tile in a diagonal pattern softens the tunnel effect of a long, narrow kitchen, making it seem wider (see the right photo below).

Can Tile Be Used as a Cutting Board?

Although few tile or stone surfaces can stand up to a sharp kitchen knife, most hold up well under other kitchen rigors such as abuse from pots and pans. Limestone scratches easily, but those scratches can be sanded out. Surfaces such as glossy tile or highly polished granite tend to show marks more readily, and their scratches are harder to remove or cover up. Stone or ceramic tile with a matte finish tends to hide scratches and surface abrasions better.

Stone tile is also porous, so it has to be sealed properly to resist staining from things such as red wine and grease. And some ceramic tiles, as well as polished stone such as granite or marble, can lose their shine when exposed to some food acids.

As in floors, latex-modified grout should be used on tiled countertops along with a good coat of grout sealer. Again, epoxy grout, which costs a little more and is a little harder to install, will make the grout impenetrable.

Should the Backsplash Blend or Make a Splash?

A tile backsplash is the spot where you can be really creative with tile in the kitchen (see the photos on p. 94). Because a backsplash functions to protect the wall from splashes and splatters that come from cooking and preparing food, the only prerequisite is that backsplash tile be easy to keep clean. Beyond that, the choices become mainly aesthetic.

I always ask clients how much stuff they plan to keep on their countertops. Toasters, microwaves, and canisters tend to block the backsplash, and in that case, the backsplash just provides a backdrop of color and tex-

Sources

Miracle Sealants Company
800-350-1901
www.miraclesealants.com
Porous Plus

One Master Marble and Stone Care
760-406-1097
www.onemastermarble.com
Gold Shield

The Tile Council of America
864-646-8453
www.tileusa.com

ture. I usually recommend extending the tile from the countertop all the way to the bottoms of the wall cabinets so that the backsplash acts as a visual connection between the upper and lower cabinets.

Borders usually work best above long stretches of counter that are uninterrupted by windows or appliances. And when installed three-quarters of the way up the backsplash, a border won't get lost near the countertop or under the wall cabinets. At that height, a border will usually clear the height of the toaster or a bowl of fruit for a continuous line.

If the client is thinking of having decorative tiles scattered randomly throughout the backsplash, I suggest taping playing cards to the wall at random to see if the effect works in that particular kitchen. Playing cards can also be used in a line to test the visual power of a border.

Isn't Tile Expensive?

Tile varies greatly in price, and budget is a concern for the vast majority of my clients. So here's my strategy for keeping costs down. First, use reasonably priced machine-made tile for large areas in the kitchen. Then there will be money left for those handmade borders, small murals, or strategically placed accent tiles that will give your kitchen a rich look without breaking the bank (see the right photo below).

Installation prices can vary greatly depending on the type of tile, the layout, and the conditions of the existing floors and walls. A tile installer can explain what your options are and how much each option costs. Even if you opt for a less expensive installation, always seal the tile. Sealing tile is pretty easy, so you can save a little by doing it yourself. Spend some money on a good sealer.

Lane Meehan is a tile maker and designer of decorative tiles. She and her husband, Tom, own and manage Cape Cod Tileworks in Harwich, Massachusetts.

Tile Art and Accents

The backsplash of cows in a pasture (see the left photo below) in this kitchen designed by Randy Fritz of Lakeside, Calif., combines the art of Roger Dunham of Petaluma, Calif., with the practicality of ceramic tile. Random decorative tiles in a backsplash of less expensive, machine-made tile (see the right photo below) give this kitchen a colorful accent.

Tiling a Kitchen Counter

■ BY DENNIS HOURANY

It took two days to complete my first shower, including the time I spent at the library reading up on how to do it. That was 26 years ago. Since then, I've laid hundreds of tile floors and counters. My San Francisco-area tile contracting company often works in housing developments, where a journeyman tilesetter with only one helper can set a tile counter in a single day. Even if you don't set as much tile as we do, installing a kitchen counter should be a straightforward and relatively speedy process.

Tile can be set on either a mortar bed or cement board (see the photos on p. 96). Around here, counters are almost always set on a mortar bed ¾ in. thick. I think that produces the best tile job—it's strong, durable and easily leveled. Whichever substrate you choose, the processes of laying out the counter and installing the tile are identical.

Before you put down either cement board or a mortar bed, make sure you have a solid wood base on top of the cabinets. I use a ¾-in., exterior-grade plywood (although you can also use 1x6 boards with ¼-in. gaps between them). If you use plywood, it's a good idea to make a series of cuts through the sheet with a circular saw to prevent the rough top from warping. Snap a series of

parallel lines 6 in. to 8 in. apart along the length of the plywood, then make 6-in.- to 8-in.-long cuts along the lines, leaving 6 in. to 8 in. between them. Where overhangs are larger than about 8 in., you must provide

A Tile Counter Built to Last

Tile makes a long-wearing and attractive surface for a kitchen counter. Whether the tile is set on a mortar bed, as it is here, or on a layer of cement board, a trouble-free installation starts with a wood rough top that has been securely fastened to the cabinet base. Thinset adhesive bonds the tile to the mortar bed.

Field tile
V-cap tile
Thinset adhesive
Mortar bed
Wire reinforcement
Cap metal
Moisture barrier
¾-in. exterior-grade plywood screwed to cabinet

Don't get hung up on the substrate. The author starts a tiled kitchen counter with a mortar bed (see the left photo above), but you don't have to. Cement board (see the right photo above) is another choice. For more on cement board, see "Cement Board Is a Quick Alternative to a Mortar Bed" on pp. 100–101.

TIP

Outside cooking areas are becoming quite common and this method of installation could also be used for a counter installation in an outdoor kitchen.

adequate support—with corbels, for example—to prevent movement in the plywood that would crack the tile or grout.

Protect Cabinets from Moisture

Mortar is wet stuff, so we install a moisture barrier over the rough top of the cabinet. You may use an asphalt-impregnated paper, such as 30–30 kraft paper, 15-lb. roofing felt or 4-mil polyethylene film. When we staple the material to the rough top, we let it hang all the way to the floor to protect the cabinets as we install tile. Excess paper can be trimmed away later. Paper should cover all rough-top edges, including those around the sink cutout and any other openings. Seams should be lapped at least 2 in. If you are installing backsplash tiles over a mortar bed, extend the paper up the wall beyond where the tile will end to protect the wall. Or use masking tape to protect untiled areas of the wall above the backsplash.

A mortar bed should be reinforced with some kind of metal lath. The kind approved by the Tile Council of America is a galvanized, expanded type that should weigh at least 2½ lb. per sq. yd. We use 1-in., 20-ga.

galvanized stucco netting or chicken wire. I like to run the wire on the deck and up the wall to within ½ in. of where the tile will stop, provided the backsplash tile does not extend up the wall more than roughly 8 in. If your plan is to carry the tile all the way to the bottom of the upper cabinets, then cut the wire at the juncture between deck and backsplash and install a separate piece of wire on the wall.

We staple the wire every 4 in. to 6 in. with staples at least ⅜ in. long. After the wire comes cap metal, which supports the perimeter of the mortar bed and is used as a guide to screed the surface (see photo 2 on the facing page). Cap metal comes in a variety of shapes and sizes. We typically finish counter edges with a piece of tile called V-cap, which forms a 90-degree tile corner, so our cap metal is usually the J-cap variety. You can get cap metal at tile-supply houses or at some of the super hardware stores.

One big advantage of a mortar bed is that you can provide a level surface for tile even if the cabinets are not quite level—something that's harder to do when you're using cement board. So make sure the top edge of the cap metal is level before you start snugging up the nails and fixing the cap in place (see photo 3 on the facing page).

Readying Cabinets for a Mortar Bed

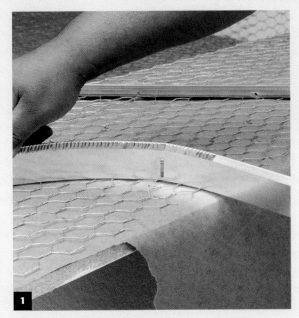

1 Getting the kinks out. To avoid kinks in the cap metal where it goes around a curve in the counter's edge, make a series of cuts in the top edge at the bend with a pair of aviation snips.

2 Cap metal supports the mortar. Elite Tile's Ernie Grijalva loosely nails cap metal to the edge of a counter. Moisture-resistant, asphalt-impregnated kraft paper protects the plywood.

3 Level the metal. Once the cap metal has been leveled, Grijalva drives the nails home. By keeping the top edge of the cap metal 3/4 in. above the top, he knows the counter will be thick enough at any point.

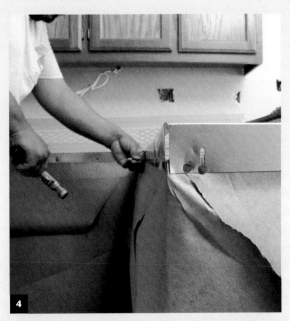

4 A second nail for insurance. Slots in the cap metal allow it to be adjusted up and down for level. Once leveled, the cap metal is anchored with a second nail driven right through the metal.

Two Kinds of Mortar Make a Bed That Can Be Tiled the Same Day

We use two types of mortar in a counter: fat mud and deck mud. Because it contains lime, fat mud is sticky enough to adhere to vertical surfaces. For most horizontal surfaces, we use deck mud, a much drier mix that's not as susceptible to shrinking or cracking.

Fat mud (no, I'm not sure how it got its name) is a mixture of 5 parts plaster sand, 1 part portland cement, and 1 part type-S or comparable lime. These three ingredients are mixed thoroughly before clean water is added. Consistency is crucial. If the mortar is too wet, it won't stay on the trowel. If it's too dry, it won't stick to the wall.

We mix a batch of this mortar first, but before applying any of it, we install wooden screed strips on vertical surfaces to determine the depth of the mud bed. Make the strips ½ in. thick and nail them right to the wall over the wire. We use 1½-in. drywall nails, which are easy to pull out later; avoid nailing the screed to a stud. Screed strips should be placed near edges and at intervals so that you will be able to span the distance between them with a straightedge.

We work fat mud firmly into the chicken wire on all vertical surfaces. This is called a scratch coat, and it's essential for getting the rest of the mortar bed to stay put. We bank fat mud against all the cap metal along outside edges, from the top of the metal down to the deck at about a 45-degree angle. Finally, fat mud is used around all deck penetrations, such as the sink cutout, because it holds its shape there better than deck mud (see the bottom left photo on the facing page).

After troweling a generous layer of fat mud on the backsplash area, we use a length of straight aluminum or wood to screed the surface and then fill any low spots and screed again. At this point, we remove the screed strips that were nailed to the wall and gently fill in the voids with mortar. Any excess may be cut away once the mortar has firmed up.

Deck mud is used to fill in the remainder of the countertop. It consists of 5 parts sand and 1 part portland cement. Mix these ingredients thoroughly before adding water—and remember to keep the mix dry (see the top photos on the facing page). It should not ooze through your fingers. Trowel and pack down the deck mud over the deck to an elevation slightly higher than the cap metal.

We do not use wooden screeds on the countertop. Instead, we use a level to create several flat spots and then tamp in lengths of cap metal to guide the aluminum straightedge. Locations for these screed pads are somewhat strategic. They need to be placed at all turns in the counter as well as at intermediate locations to allow the straightedge to cover the entire countertop. The cap metal at the edges of the counter also acts as a screed.

Once you have spread enough mortar on the top, use a straightedge to screed off the excess (see the bottom right photo on the facing page), fill the low spots and screed again, then remove the cap-metal pieces used as screed pads. A wooden trowel will not bring water to the surface like a metal tool will, but one last pass with a flat-edged metal trowel leaves a smoother finish.

A Few Fundamentals Help Make Tile Layout Less Complicated

Laying out individual tiles so that the job is aesthetically pleasing as a whole is no easy feat, especially in those kitchens where counters wrap around corners or make angled jogs. It is virtually a given that tiles will have to be cut somewhere. The trick is in making the cuts where they are least

Mix Two Kinds of Mortar

Deck mud is a dry mix. Add just enough water so that the mortar holds its shape when it is compressed into a ball.

Fat mud for edges and vertical surfaces. Grijalva's helper, Martin Arellano, builds a layer of fat mud along the edge of the sink cutout. The limed mortar sticks to surfaces and holds its shape.

With both types of mortar in place, Grijalva uses an aluminum straightedge to screed the countertop. One end rides on a piece of cap metal that has been leveled and tamped in the mortar.

obvious and making the tile pattern as a whole pleasing to the eye.

A few fundamentals will help. First, try to lay out the counter so that no tile you set is less than half its original size. Second, never break, or interrupt, grout lines unless you are using two different-size tiles or unless you can dramatically improve the layout by doing so. Grout lines generally should be continuous as they move from the countertop to the backsplash or up other vertical surfaces. Although it's a matter of personal preference, I look at countertop penetrations, such as a cooktop or sink, as unavoidable interruptions in the tile job as a whole—not something the tile layout should be maneuvered around.

We begin setting tiles immediately after the mortar bed has been leveled and tamped. But first, we mark out reference lines along the edges of the counter to indicate where the V-cap starts (see photo 1 on p. 102).

I start with full tiles on as many of the leading or open edges of the counter as possible (see the drawing on p. 102). Open edges are those that do not abut a restraining edge, such as a wall or a raised counter. Cut tiles should go at the back. In many of the kitchens we do, L- and U-shaped counters are common, so we are careful to start the first full tile as shown in the drawing on p. 102. This layout ensures the greatest number of full-field tiles and the fewest disruptions in the overall pattern.

Cement Board Is a Quick Alternative to a Mortar Bed

In Dennis Hourany's part of the country, the West Coast, a mortar bed is usually specified as the substrate for a tiled kitchen counter. But tilesetters in other regions may prefer a cement-board underlayment, such as Durock or WonderBoard® (see "Sources" on p. 107). These panels, made of portland cement and reinforcing fiberglass mesh, speed up preparation of the tile substrate considerably.

For Tom Meehan, a tilesetter in Harwich, Massachusetts, cement board is the substrate of choice for kitchen counters (see the drawing below). It bonds well with the thinset adhesive used to set the tile, and it can be installed quickly.

Cement board is fairly easy to cut (see photos 1–3 on the facing page). Treat the material like drywall—score a line with a utility knife a few times, snap the board along the line, and then cut the back of the board along the break. You can get a smoother cut with a circular saw and carbide blade, but be careful. Breathing the dust is unhealthy. Meehan suggests cutting the board outside and making sure you wear a respirator.

Before installing the cement board, Meehan screws down a layer of 3/4-in. exterior-grade plywood on the top of the cabinet. Screw heads should be flush with the surface. Next is a layer of thinset mortar or construction adhesive (see photo 4 on the facing page), followed by 1/2-in.-thick cement board.

If you're using construction adhesive, work quickly because it begins to skim over in about five minutes and loses its pliability.

Meehan presses the cement board into place and jiggles it gently to even out the adhesive beneath it. The cement board is attached with 1 1/4-in. galvanized drywall screws 8 in. on center (see photo 5 on the facing page). You may want to drill pilot holes.

If kitchen cabinets already have laminate counters that are structurally sound, you can leave them in place and put down 1/4-in. or 5/16-in. cement board right on top of the laminate. Laminate should be scuffed with a 50-grit sandpaper first. The total substrate should be no less than 1 1/4 in. thick.

Edges can be handled a couple of ways. In the installation featured here, Meehan brings the cement board flush to the edge of the plywood and then finishes the edge with a layer of thinset and fiberglass mesh tape (see photo 6 on the facing page). Another approach is to finish the outside edge with a vertical strip of cement board, and then apply a layer of thinset and mesh tape.

Cement board is available in thicknesses of 1/4 in., 5/16 in., 7/16 in., 1/2 in. and 5/8 in. Sheets may be 32 in., 36 in., or 48 in. wide.

Although Meehan thinks cement board is best, another possibility is a material called DensShield

Cement Board Makes a Good Bond with Thinset Adhesive

Applying 1/2-in. cement board over a layer of 3/4-in. exterior-grade plywood makes a stable substrate for a tiled kitchen counter. It's faster to install than a traditional mortar bed.

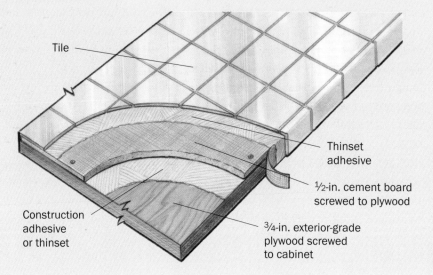

Tile

Thinset adhesive

1/2-in. cement board screwed to plywood

3/4-in. exterior-grade plywood screwed to cabinet

Construction adhesive or thinset

1 Score cement board with a knife. Tilesetter Tom Meehan uses a utility knife and a straightedge to score a piece of Durock cement board.

3 The board should break cleanly. Once fibers on the back of the board have been severed, the sheet should break cleanly along the score line.

4 Bond the cement board to the counter. A bead of construction adhesive may be used to bond the cement board to the rough top.

Score the back, too. After snapping the cement board along the score line, Meehan cuts through the back of the sheet, like working with drywall.

5 Screws hold the cement board down. Galvanized drywall screws 8 in. o.c. keep the cement board in place while the adhesive sets up.

made by Georgia-Pacific (see "Sources" on p. 107), which was recommended by a number of *Fine Homebuilding* readers on "Breaktime," the magazine's web discussion group (www.finehomebuilding.com). Georgia-Pacific says DensShield is one-third lighter than portland-cement backerboard and is more water resistant than cement-board products. The company says the board has a proprietary heat-cured surface with a silicone-treated core embedded with glass mats.

Scott Gibson is a contributing writer to Fine Homebuilding *and coauthored* Toward a Zero Energy Home *(The Taunton Press, Inc., 2010).*

6 Finish edges with thinset. Fiberglass mesh tape and a thin layer of thinset adhesive finish the edges. This substrate is now ready for tile.

Tile-Layout Basics

Keep Cut Tiles at the Back of the Counter

In this counter of 6x6 tile, layout starts with control lines showing where field tiles end and V-cap starts. The first full tile is set at the intersection of two control lines. Where possible, cut tiles are kept at the back of the counter.

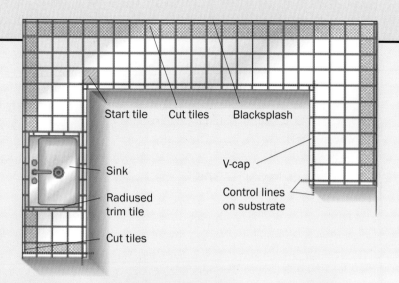

Start tile   Cut tiles   Blacksplash

Sink

Radiused trim tile

Cut tiles

V-cap

Control lines on substrate

Ready for layout. With the mortar bed tamped and leveled, a piece of V-cap is used to set layout lines. Grijalva uses a utility knife to mark the inside edge.

Snap lines around the perimeter. After marking all counter edges with the V-cap, Grijalva and his helper snap chalklines. These control lines are essential for setting straight courses of field tile.

Keep grout lines straight. When turning a corner, a framing square prevents wandering grout lines. If tile is being set over a mortar bed before it is cured, be careful not to mar the surface.

A straightedge makes diagonal cuts easier. Grijalva lays dry tile on the mortar bed, then marks the tile with a straightedge. After the tiles have been cut, thinset and tile are brought to the layout line.

Tile-Setting Compound: Thinset vs. Mastic

Over the years, I've laid tile using both mastic and thinset. Each was around long before I cut my first tile, and each has proved to be a sound material when used appropriately.

The easiest way isn't always the best. Thinset must be mixed on site and isn't as tacky as mastic. However, thinset provides a better-performing bond between tile and substrate.

Thinset is stronger and more versatile

All thinset is cementitious, which gives it far greater shear and tensile strength than mastic. This quality greatly expands where thinset can and should be used. Because thinset cures as hard and as strong as the cement backerboard it's often adhered to, it is the best material to use when setting tile in demanding conditions: in steam rooms and on floors, shower walls, and ceilings. It even holds up exceptionally well outdoors.

Thinset isn't as tacky as mastic, so it's easier to adjust a tile layout as you go. It also means that tiles can slip and sag more easily, which is always a concern on vertical and ceiling installations.

Mastic has fewer uses, but it's easier to work with

Mastic is organic glue mixed with additives that give it body, so it can be troweled and textured like thinset. Unlike thinset, which is mixed on site, mastic is ready to use straight out of the bucket. I use mastic for tile backsplashes and tile wainscot because of its great tack and nonslip qualities. I even use it in hot-tub surrounds if I know it won't be exposed to a lot of water.

Mastic's bonding strength can be greatly reduced when exposed to water, and it can also sustain mold growth. Another drawback is that mastic cures by evaporation, so when applied too thickly or on large tiles, the adhesive can take a long time to cure—if it cures at all. Also, mastic should never be used on stone tiles because it can be absorbed into the material and cause surface staining.

Tom Meehan is a second-generation tile installer who has been installing tile for more than 35 years. Tom lives with his wife, Lane, and their four sons in Harwich, Massachusetts, where they own Cape Cod Tileworks.

It would be impossible to cover all the layout problems you may have to wrestle with. For this reason, consider using a story pole, which you can make yourself. Lay tiles in a row on the floor with the desired grout spacing. Place a length of wood alongside these tiles, and mark it where tiles fall. You can place the story pole at any point on the area to be tiled and see right away what your cuts will look like. If you're tiling for someone other than yourself, it may be best to involve him or her in layout decisions, and a story pole can be a big help in explaining the options. You also can simply lay out tiles to test a pattern, but a story pole is faster. You may find that starting the tile in a different spot yields the best overall countertop pattern with the fewest awkward cuts.

Inside Angles Call For Mitered Edge Pieces

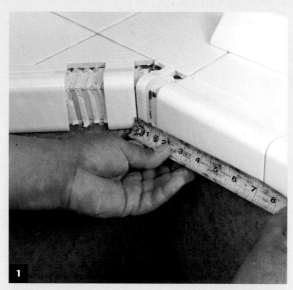

Use scrap to find the inside corner. Mitering the two pieces of V-cap meeting in this 45-degree corner will make the neatest job. To start, Grijalva uses two offcuts to establish the corner, then measures for the first mitered piece of V-cap.

Eye the cut on a tile saw. By aligning one pencil mark on the slot in the saw's sliding table and the other mark with the blade, you can make an accurate miter cut on a tile saw.

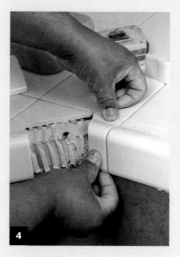

One down, one to go. This piece of mitered V-cap fits the space perfectly, but it's safer to dry-fit both pieces before applying any mastic.

Smooth edges for a seamless job. For all exposed edges that must be cut, a tile saw followed by a pumice stone gives a much smoother finish than a snap cutter. Use a snap cutter where tile edges will be buried.

Now fit the second piece. With the first mitered section in place, Grijalva can mark and cut the second piece of V-cap. The result is a neat, well-fitting corner.

Sinks can be handled in several ways. One option is to set a self-rimming sink on top of the field tile once the counter is done. For a neater appearance, set the sink in the mortar bed before field tile is laid, then use trim tiles with a radiused edge as a border.

Field Tiles Are Set in an Even Layer of Thinset Adhesive

The adhesive used to bond tile to either a mortar bed or cement board is called dry-set mortar or thinset. We use basic thinset on ceramic and other pervious tiles. Latex- or polymer-modified thinset is a good choice for impervious tile such as porcelain. Instructions printed on the bag will tell you which size notched trowel to use and how to apply the thinset. It is crucial to follow the instructions exactly. You should mix only enough thinset that can be tiled over within 15 minutes. Don't let it skim over.

The only spot where we don't use thinset is on the edges where V-cap tiles are installed. We have seen these tiles crack when thinset is used, possibly because the thinset makes a rigid bond that's tough on the 90-degree edge of the V-cap if there's any flex in the rough top. We now use premixed tile mastic for these edge pieces. Mastic stays more pliable than thinset, and the edge tiles don't crack.

Thinset should not ooze up more than two-thirds of the way into the grout joint. If that seems to be happening, you may be using a trowel with too deep a notch or you may not be applying a consistent amount of thinset. When you get too much thinset in a joint, simply rake it out.

We start with a full tile at the intersection of control lines on the countertop. Many tiles are produced with spacers, called lugs, on the edges. You can set the tiles together or space them farther apart, but never wider than the thickness of the tile so that the grout won't crack. To help keep the joints consistent if the spacing is greater than the lugs provide, you can use plastic spacers available where you buy tile.

But don't count on spacers to keep the lines straight—that is what control lines and straightedges are for. A framing square helps keep tiles aligned when turning corners (see the photo 3 on p. 102), and aluminum angle

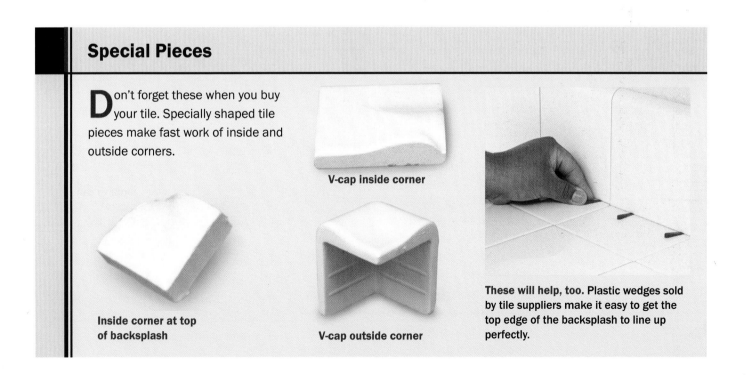

Special Pieces

Don't forget these when you buy your tile. Specially shaped tile pieces make fast work of inside and outside corners.

V-cap inside corner

Inside corner at top of backsplash

V-cap outside corner

These will help, too. Plastic wedges sold by tile suppliers make it easy to get the top edge of the backsplash to line up perfectly.

Radiused Corners Need Special Fitting

Grijalva pencils in the line where a field tile will have to be cut to fit a radiused corner. He cuts the curves on a tile saw by nibbling to the line. Pie-shaped pieces of V-cap, cut by eye and tested until they fit, complete the corner.

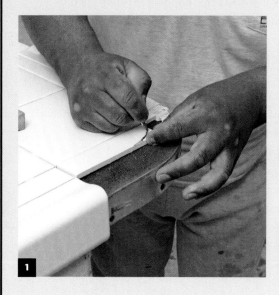

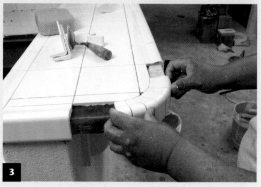

stock is invaluable for staying on track—we keep several different lengths on all our jobs. A good alternative is a straight piece of wood.

Some counter shapes require a number of tiles to be cut on a diagonal at the counter edge (see photo 4 on p. 102). In these situations, we lay these tiles out dry (no thinset) so that they can be marked with a pencil and straightedge. Once the tiles are cut on a tile saw, the thinset can be troweled on and the tiles set in place. Inside corners and curved edges can be tricky, but they are easily managed with a little care (see "Inside Angles Call for Mitered Edged Pieces" on p. 104).

A tile saw is indispensable. Rent one if you can't find a friend who will loan you one. A saw produces a clean cut that needs only a little touch up with a pumice stone. Snap cutters are faster, but the edge isn't smooth enough to be shown on the finished counter. We use snap cutters when the edge will be buried, such as at the back of the counter where the backsplash hides any roughness. And when you pick up your tile supplies, make sure you ask for plastic wedges and corner pieces (see "Special Pieces" on p. 105).

Grouting Is the Final Step

Grouting is easy if you follow two simple rules. First, use the proper tools—a smooth, hard-rubber grout float and top-quality hydro sponges. Second, and most important, follow the grout manufacturer's instructions. Even the best tools can't salvage a job when the grout has been mixed or applied improperly. Tile adhesive should cure for at least 24 hours before grout is applied. Before getting started, remove any loose material from the joints. You also may want to apply a grout release to the surface of unglazed tiles to prevent staining.

Grout stays workable for about two hours. You should restir the grout mix periodically as you work, but do not add any more liquid to it. If the grout becomes too stiff to work, throw it out and make a fresh batch.

Once the grout is mixed and you've removed any debris from the joints, use the hard-rubber float to force grout into the joints (see photo 1 below). Work diagonally using enough pressure to ensure the joints are filled. Then remove excess grout with the edge of the float. After allowing the grout to set up for 15 minutes or so, wet and ring out a sponge and wipe the tile diagonally (see photo 2 below).

For your final pass, use each side of the sponge only once before rinsing it out. You can use a soft, dry cloth to polish off the haze that forms after about 40 minutes (see photo 3 below). Misting the grout with water several times a day for two or three days will increase its strength and prevent cracking. But wait 10 days before applying any grout sealer—an important step that increases water and stain resistance.

Dennis Hourany owns Elite Tile in Walnut Creek, California.

Sources

Custom Building Products
800-272-8786
www.custombuildingproducts.com
WonderBoard

Georgia-Pacific
800-225-6119
www.gp.com
DensShield

USG
800-874-4968
www.usg.com
Durock

Finishing Up

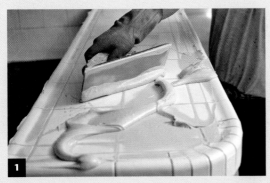

1 Wait a day before grouting. Once the thinset has cured, mix grout to a creamy consistency and force the material into the gaps between tiles with a hard-rubber float. Work the float at an angle.

2 Keep the sponge clean. A tile sponge cleans up the residue. Be careful not to dig out any grout, and rinse the sponge frequently.

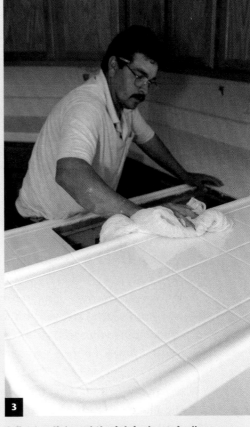

3 A final polish and the job is done. Arellano uses a generous pad of clean cheesecloth to remove the haze left by the tile sponge. The surface polishes quickly.

Tiling over a Laminate Counter

■ BY DAVID HART

I tear out tons of tub surrounds and sheet vinyl every year and install ceramic tile. That type of remodeling makes up the bulk of my work. Other than an occasional mud-set floor, I use cementitious backerboard as tile underlayment on walls and floors. After having mixed results with plywood, I found that backerboard also works great for countertop renovations.

The major advantage to installing backer-board over an existing laminate countertop is that it keeps down the total cost of the tile installation. Instead of building a new countertop, I set the tile on a sheet of ¼-in. backerboard that's screwed to the old laminate. The backerboard provides a sturdy, stable substrate for the tile; it saves me a day (or more) of labor; and it can knock several hundred dollars off the total cost of the project. (Obviously, this method won't work on postformed counters.)

Why not install the tile directly on the countertop? It doesn't work. I learned the hard way that latex- and polymer-modified thinsets don't bond well to plastic laminate, even though a mortar manufacturer assured me that they would. After two installation failures involving only thinset, I now overlay the laminate with backerboard and haven't had a callback since.

Make Sure the Original Counter Is Sound

Because a new sink is often part of a counter renovation, my first step is to determine the size of the new sink cutout. If the new sink is smaller than the original, I have to rebuild the counter to give the sink proper support before overlaying the top with backerboard. If the new sink dimensions are larger, I cut the countertop to the correct size and continue with the installation. (It's also worth noting here that unless they have flexible water supplies, most sinks need to be replumbed due to the increased depth of the counter.)

Cut and Fit the Backerboard

Cutting backerboard with a grinder is dusty but quick. Although backerboard can be scored with a utility knife and snapped, an angle grinder fitted with a diamond blade cuts a cleaner line faster.

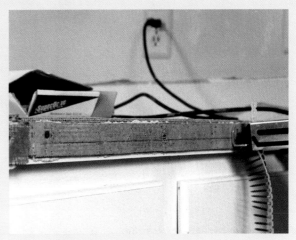

Narrower edge strips are more easily concealed. To ensure that the tile covers the backerboard, the author keeps the edge strips at least ¼ in. back from the counter's edge.

I also check the condition of the counter's particleboard. Prolonged exposure to steam from a dishwasher or water seepage from around the sink can turn particleboard into little more than loose sawdust. The best way to check is to crawl into the base cabinet and examine the underside of the countertop with a flashlight. If I can dig particleboard apart with a screwdriver or pocketknife or if it's swelling from exposure to moisture, then the damage is probably too severe to use this installation method. Scrap the existing top, rebuild it, and quit reading this chapter.

All laminate countertops will move when you pound a fist on them, but excessive movement will lead to cracked grout joints and, eventually, loose tiles. Cement backerboards help tighten any floor or countertop if installed properly, but bouncy or spongy tops need to be fixed or scrapped. Often, a few screws driven up into the countertop through the cabinets' corner brackets will stiffen a bouncy top.

It's also important at this early stage to measure the height of the tiles that cover the edge of the counter (called V-cap) and compare that dimension to the height of the countertop's finished edge. The V-cap should cover the countertop edge and backerboard. A typical V-cap covers about 1¾ in., which doesn't leave much tile hanging below the substrate; some run deeper, and others run a little shallower. I also make sure the cabinet drawers don't hit the tile overhang.

Cutting Cement Backerboard

If I need to keep the job site clean, sometimes I cut backerboard with a utility knife and a straightedge. Although it's slightly more expensive than other backerboard, Durock (see "Sources" on p. 112) is somewhat softer and easier to cut with a standard utility knife. Yes, I burn through blades, but it's quick and virtually dust-free.

Glue and Screw to the Countertop

Thinset increases the bond. Like peanut butter spread between two pieces of bread, thinset troweled onto the counter will fill voids beneath the backerboard and strengthen the substrate.

An autofeed screw gun speeds a tedious job. Faced with a day of driving screws into substrate, the author uses an autofeed screw gun that starts and seats each screw much faster than by hand.

Utility knives don't work well on harder, slicker boards such as WonderBoard (see "Sources" on p. 112), so to cut those types of board, I rely on a right-angle grinder with a 4-in. dry-cut diamond blade (see the left photo on p. 109). A vital piece of equipment for compound or circular cuts as well, this tool throws a cloud of dust anytime I cut cement board with it, so I never use it in an enclosed space.

I always lay the board in place dry to check the fit; I usually allow up to a ½-in. gap between the counter and wall and up to a ¼-in. gap between individual pieces of board. The important thing here is that I don't want the backerboard to extend beyond the edges of the top. After I cut the backerboard to fit the existing top, I cut strips for the counter's edge about ¼ in. narrower than the edge of the countertop (see the right photo on p. 109) so that the backerboard doesn't stick out below the bottom of the edge cap.

Modified Thinset and Screws Make a Better Bond

By itself, ¼-in. backerboard offers no additional strength when attached directly to the substrate; a layer of the thinset beneath the backerboard fills the voids and creates a vacuum that is nearly impossible to break. I never skip this step. Unmodified mortar doesn't provide any bond to the laminate, although it will stick to the backerboard, so I always spend the few extra dollars and get latex or polymer-modified thinset, which cures harder than unmodified mortar and allows a small amount of deflection.

It's important to mix thinset with the proper amount of water. As a rule, too much water will create a weak bond; too little makes the product tough to trowel, and it may not bond to the tile or backerboard properly. I try to mix it so that it has a smooth, creamy consistency. If the mix clings to my trowel without running off and still spreads easily, then I know I've got a good mix.

After mixing a batch of thinset, I trowel it onto the counter (see the left photo on the facing page) with a ¼-in. notch trowel, trying not to spread more thinset than I can use in 10 to 15 minutes. For an experienced tilesetter, that can mean the entire counter, but for those new to this type of work, that might mean covering a small section at one time. Once a section of counter is covered, I lay the backerboard in place and screw it down.

Because the board is only ¼ in. thick, I use screws that are 1 in. long. Longer screws might protrude through the bottom of the particleboard and give someone a nasty scrape. I like to space the screws about 6 in. apart on the perimeter of the board and 8 in. to 10 in. apart on the inside. Although I have used loose screws and a screw gun, I usually rely on a Makita® (see "Sources" on p. 102) autofeed screw gun (see the right photo on the facing page); it's just quicker. I try to make sure that there are no bubbles in the backerboard and that I seat the screw heads flush or slightly below the surface.

Tile Layout: Big Tiles Are Better

Once the counter is ready, I take time for a careful tile layout. Nothing will ruin an installation more than a poor layout. For this project, I first installed the 6-in. V-caps, starting from the outside corners and working toward the wall (see the left photo below). I butter the backside of each tile as I go, which makes the next step cleaner.

Once the edge is complete, I lay out the interior tile pattern dry (see the right photo below) to see which tiles will have to be cut. On a perfect installation, I would end up with full tiles across the full width of the counter, but that never happens. The best installation will have the largest tiles possible in the most visible areas. And I'll often try to cut a small amount from tiles on both sides of the layout rather than cutting a large amount from the tiles on one side.

Test-Fit and Set the Tile

V-caps go on first. These narrow, right-angle tiles form a border for the square field tiles. Starting at the exterior bullnose corners, the V-caps are laid out in an equal pattern that ends at a wall or a mitered inside corner.

Layout starts from the center. To ensure a well-spaced layout, the author places whole tiles across the space, using a center mark as a reference. The remaining space is divided into two partial tiles.

Finish Up with Grout

Grout works best when spread in small areas. Worked into tile joints with a rubber float, grout tends to set up quickly, and it becomes difficult to remove from the tile surface. A clean, damp sponge is the best tool to wipe excess grout from tiles and to smooth grout lines.

Sources

USG
800-874-4968
www.usg.com
Durock

Custom Building Products
800-272-8786
www.custombuildingproducts.com
WonderBoard

Makita
800-462-5482
www.makita.com
Autofeed screw gun

Once I've checked the layout, I start applying enough thinset to keep me going for about 10 minutes. If the mix sits on the backerboard for much longer than that, it starts to skim over, and then it won't bond with the tile.

Apply Small Areas of Grout

After the tile is set, I wait a day for the thinset to cure before I start grouting. Most grout has a modifier in it, which creates a stronger, more stain-resistant grout, so there's no need to add latex to the dry powder. The grout–water mix should be stiffer than toothpaste but loose enough to push across the tile without great force.

Using a rubber float, I usually won't spread more grout than I can work in about 10 minutes (see the left photo above). I don't allow the grout to sit on the tile surface for long, either; once it has hardened, the grout is difficult to remove. I use a large damp sponge to smooth the joints and to wipe off the face of the tile (see the right photo above). It's important not to wipe too much out of the joints, to rinse the sponge frequently, and to wring the excess water out of the sponge. Too much water can discolor or weaken grout.

David Hart is a tile contractor and outdoors writer living in Rice, Virginia.

Tiling a Backsplash

■ BY TOM MEEHAN

Tile transformation. A tile backsplash can lift an ordinary kitchen to extraordinary heights. Here, tumbled marble is the perfect complement to granite countertops and cherry cabinets.

Saturday is estimate day at our store, Cape Cod Tileworks. Of the five or six estimates we do on Saturday mornings, at least a third of them are for kitchen backsplashes. Whether the room is new or old, a backsplash is a great opportunity to express a kitchen's qualities, including color, creativity, boldness, subtlety, and craftsmanship. If you haven't done a lot of tiling, a backsplash is a great way to get your feet wet.

Layout: A Road Map for the Backsplash

Once the tile has been selected, the next step is layout. For this project, my client chose tumbled-marble tile. Its coarse natural texture makes a particularly nice contrast to a smooth, shiny kitchen countertop, such as granite.

The layout for most of this backsplash is fairly simple: three courses of 4-in. by 4-in. tile topped off by a narrow border; a filler course takes care of the space between the border and the wall cabinets. The challenging part is the patterned area behind the stove. Taller and more intricate than the rest of the backsplash, this area requires a layout that is dead-on accurate. My first step is measuring the exact dimensions of that space.

Over the years, I've found that doing the layout directly on the wall doesn't work well. Instead, I draw a full-size layout of the patterned area on a sheet of cardboard. Then I cut and arrange all the tiles as needed to fit the layout. I don't start to set tile on the wall until the test-fit is complete. This backsplash features small square dots at the intersections of the diamonds. At this point, I mark and cut these types of elements as well.

If a backsplash is interrupted by a window, it looks best if the tiles on each side of the window are the same size, which often means using partial tiles elsewhere. I plan

Test-fit the tiles on a flat surface. For the area above the stove, the author first measures the exact dimensions (photo 1). Then he transfers them to a sheet of cardboard, where all the tile is dry-fit. Decorative elements such as the border and the square accent tiles are cut and fit at this time (photos 2 and 3).

Trowel on the mastic. White mastic is the adhesive of choice for this project because a darker color might show through the light-colored tile. The entire backsplash is spread before any tile is set.

the size and location of these partial tiles to please the eye.

Electrical outlets have to be incorporated into most backsplashes. A symmetrical layout around an electrical box looks best and is the easiest to cut (see "Working Around an Electrical Outlet" on p. 117). In extreme cases, the box can be moved for a proper-looking layout.

Install the Tile in the Right Order

Before mud and mastic start flying, it's critical to protect appliances, countertops, and other finished surfaces. For this installation, a rubber shower-pan liner and a piece of cardboard protect the countertop and floors. The rubber liner is great because it can take a little impact if something is dropped on it. It also stays put, unlike a plastic drop cloth.

When I'm ready to set tile, I spread all-purpose mastic on the wall using a trowel with ¼-in. by ¼-in. notches (see the photo above). Because the tumbled marble for this backsplash is a fairly light color, I used nonstaining white mastic, which prevents the tile from spotting or darkening.

I set the bottom course of tiles for the backsplash first, after putting spacers under the tiles to keep them ⅛ in. above the counter. If the counter has to be replaced in the future, this space provides enough room to slip in the new countertop without disturbing the backsplash.

To install each tile, I press it tightly against the wall about ¼ in. from its final position, then slide it in place to ensure a tight bond.

With the bottom course in place, I turn to the trickiest part of the job, the patterned area behind the stove. Border pieces go in first. To create visual interest, I like the border to stand slightly proud of surrounding tiles, a subtle strategy that's not difficult to do. Before installing each border piece, I butter the back with mastic. When the tile is pressed in place, the extra mastic makes the border stand out slightly from the rest of the tile. Setting a few of the regular backsplash tiles outside the border helps keep the border pieces straight.

As I place tiles, I make the grout joints roughly ¼ in. wide. Because these tiles are irregular, the joint size varies somewhat. Instead of relying on spacers, I shift the tiles slightly as the different sizes require.

For the diamond pattern of the backsplash, I install the tiles in a diagonal sequence to keep them aligned along their longest straight edge. The tiny square accent pieces go in as I set the larger diamond tiles.

Once the stove backsplash is done, the rest of the job goes quickly. The main backsplash is only four courses high, and it's fairly easy to keep the grout lines level and straight.

As for the cut tiles that fit against the end walls and upper cabinets, I cut them for a tight fit with little or no grout joint. Grout is most likely to crack where different materials meet.

Seal the Tile before Grouting

I leave the tile overnight to let the mastic set up. The next day, I wipe down the backsplash with a good impregnator/sealer, which helps protect the marble and acts as a grout release. Grouting tumbled-marble tile is a little more difficult than grouting standard glazed tile. Grout tends to catch and collect along the irregular edges and on the surface of tumbled marble as well as in the relief of the border tiles.

I always use sanded grout with tumbled marble. Sand mixes with portland cement to add body and strength to the grout, making it superior at filling the wide joints between

Start at the border. To make the border tiles stand slightly proud of the rest of the tile, the backs receive a coat of mastic first (photo 1). This will cause the tiles to stand out from the rest of the field when they're pressed into place (photo 2).

To install a tile, press it against the wall and slide it about ¼ in. into position. Align diamond-shaped tiles along their long edges (photo 3).

Working Around an Electrical Outlet

Symmetrical coverage looks best when tile meets an electrical box. Mark the edges of the box on surrounding tiles and cut them to fit.

Cut the tile so that the ears on the outlets and the switches overlap the edges of the tile. Before installing the tiles around the box, back out the screws that secure the outlets and switches. Longer screws may be necessary to make up for the added thickness of the tile.

irregular tile edges. Border tiles like the ones in this project also demand a stronger grout because they sit farther out than the rest of the tile.

I mix a stiff but workable batch of grout that won't fall out of the joints as I float it on in a generous coat. When all the joints are filled, I let the grout sit until it is firm to the touch, usually 15 minutes or so. Then I wipe the tile with a grout sponge dampened with clean water. I make sure to wring out the sponge before wiping the tile; too much water can dissolve the cement and weaken the grout. When cleaning marble tiles, I pay extra attention to rough spots in the marble and to the patterned areas in the border tiles. These areas may need a little more effort to remove excess grout.

After washing it, I let the grout set up for another 15 minutes (less, if the room is warmer than normal). Then I use a clean terry-cloth towel to wipe the grout haze off the tile surface. At this point, I also use a putty knife to remove any grout stuck in corners or in other places where I want to see a clean, straight grout line.

The next day, I do a final cleaning with a good tile cleaner. Because some cleaners corrode or stain, I keep the countertop, stove and sink protected. A day or two after cleaning, I finish the job by applying sealer to the tile and grout. If the tile is stone (as in this case) and I sealed the tile before grouting, an additional coat of sealer also protects the grout. I apply the sealer with a disposable foam brush and give the backsplash behind the stove a couple of extra coats to protect the tile and grout from grease.

Tom Meehan is a second-generation tile installer who has been installing tile for more than 35 years. Tom lives with his wife, Lane, and their four sons in Harwich, Massachusetts, where they own Cape Cod Tileworks.

Details from Great Kitchens

Farmhouse flair. A backsplash of antiqued jade tile takes this farmhouse kitchen in Shelburne, Vermont, from predictable to posh.

A strong base. Stone floor tiles anchor this light-filled open kitchen in Alexandria, Virginia.

Classic and affordable. A ceramic subway-tile backsplash and floor of Mexican Saltillo tile revamped this kitchen while keeping it under budget.

A splash of color. This kitchen's focal point is a playful backsplash of colored tiles.

Lighten up. The iridescent glass-mosaic tiles of this backsplash reflect the undercabinet lighting, magnifying its effects.

Spice up the kitchen. An elaborate tile backsplash brings some exotic flair to an otherwise modern kitchen.

Updated retro. In this restoration, everything from the cabinetry to the tile for the backsplash was picked with an eye to creating a period-authentic bungalow kitchen with modern charm.

Mix it up. A wall of round mosaic tile in shades of yellow and green is an unexpected touch that adds plenty of fun and color to this otherwise stark white kitchen.

Buying or Renting Tile Saws

■ BY TOM MEEHAN

When I started my tile company in the 1970s, I spent $800 on a heavy-duty tub-style tile saw. It wasn't flashy and didn't have any bells and whistles, but it was the best tool at the time.

Thirty years later, prices haven't risen all that much, but the options are incredible. There are saws that run smoothly enough to make clean cuts in glass tile and others that are powerful enough to bulldoze through miles of granite without popping a circuit breaker. Some tile saws excel at accurate bevel cuts, and others are indispensable for making plunge cuts or creating curves.

The fact is that there are a number of well-made, modern tile saws that allow inexperienced tilesetters to complete projects that took old-timers years to perfect. But the trou-

ble with any market that becomes flooded with options is more difficulty in making the best choice. You can ask the clerk behind the rental desk at the local home center which saw is right for your project, but chances are that the clerk's insights reach only as far as the saw or saws in stock.

I have been in the tile business for more than half my life, have always had three or four installers on my crew, have owned more than 25 saws, and have tried countless others. The following questions and answers cover what I think are the most important features and differences in modern tile saws. Of course, no single saw does everything perfectly, but knowing the saws' strengths and weaknesses makes it easier when choosing the right one for your next project.

Cut carefully. In 30 years of installing tile, I've never seen anybody cut by a tile-saw blade, but that doesn't mean it can't happen. Treat these tools with the same caution as you would any power tool, and make sure to wear safety glasses to protect against flying tile chips.

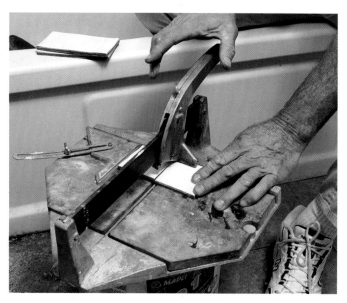

Q Do I need a tile saw at all, or can I do the job with a score-and-snap tile cutter?

A I use a snap cutter as often as possible. They are inexpensive, quick, clean, quiet, and dry. My favorite ones are made by Superior Tile Cutter®. The trouble is that this type of tool doesn't work with all varieties of tile—it is best suited for ceramics—and it can make only continuous straight cuts. You'll need a wet saw any time you have to cut around electrical outlets, vent registers, and plumbing penetrations.

Beyond Cutting Curves

The Gemini Revolution XT is no longer just a specialty saw that makes cuts that no other saw can—it has now been modified to be an everyday cutting saw. Gemini has developed a sliding table that glides on rails with the help of magnets. While I still would use a large standard saw on big porcelain tile jobs where power and speed is the key, on smaller and detailed jobs like backsplashes, the Revolution XT does it all.

The Revolution XT's ½-hp motor drives a 10-in. ring-shaped diamond blade that cuts curves in tile, porcelain, granite, and glass. The cuts are so smooth that finished edges are almost polished. It's also great for cutting notches around door jambs and toilets.

Beneath the saw table, the Revolution XT has a water bath that holds 3 gal. of water, cooling the blade and moistening fine dust. The saw is fairly quiet, it's straightforward to use, and it cuts quickly. After only a half-hour, I became really comfortable using

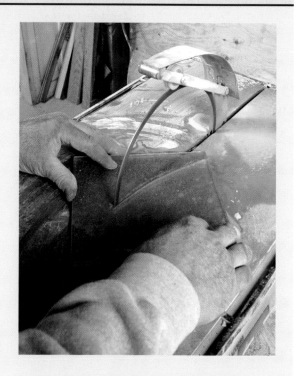

it. And even though the Revolution is not cheap, it pays for itself quickly. The saw is available all around the country and makes anyone work like a pro.

Q I want to tile the floor in my master bathroom with granite tiles set in a diagonal pattern. Can the necessary cuts be made on any wet saw?

A Granite is one of the hardest tiles, and a diagonal pattern means that every tile on the perimeter of the room needs to be cut in half. Most wet saws can muscle through hard tile, but models with small motors will bog down, have you running back and forth to reset popped circuit breakers, and burn out prematurely. Look for a saw that has a motor with at least 1½ hp (continuous, not peak). My choice for a full day of hard cutting of big tiles is the Husqvarna Tilematic® TS 250.

Tile size matters, too. Although granite tiles are typically 12x12 or smaller, many saws aren't large enough to handle 18x18 or 24x24 tiles cut on the diagonal. Read the specs before you buy, or bring in a piece of tile when you go to rent a saw.

Q When I am cutting small glass or mosaic tiles, the little pieces fall into the ½-in.-wide channel in my tile saw's cutting table. Is there a better way to control these small pieces?

A You can get around this problem in two ways. One is to make cuts to small tiles before cutting them free of the rest of the sheet (see the top photo above). If they are not part of a larger sheet, make a zero-clearance cutting platform (see the bottom photo above). To do this, cut three-fourths of the way through a piece of 12x12 tile, then set this piece of tile on the wet saw's cutting platform. The cutting groove is the same width as the wet-saw blade, and I can use a Speed® Square or another piece of tile to keep the small pieces square when sliding the table to make cuts. If you don't want to bother with jigs, consider the Gemini Revolution XT, which has a zero-clearance throat insert.

Q I have to make holes in the center of several tiles for electrical outlets. Can I use a wet saw to make these cuts?

A Yes. The safest way to make a cut in the center of a tile is by using a tile saw such as the DeWalt® D24000 or the Ridgid® R4010 with a plunge function, which allows the sawblade to be lowered into the tile. Just as with U-shaped cuts (see p. 130), plunge cuts should be made from the back of the saw, and you should account for the curve of the blade. If the desired cut must be straight and neat—which is the case for an electrical outlet—I trace it and make one cut for each side of the opening.

If the opening is small or won't be seen, I make a series of plunge cuts from the back side, stopping just shy of the face of the tile. After I've made several cuts in each direction, I tap the front side of the tile with the end of a chisel to create the opening.

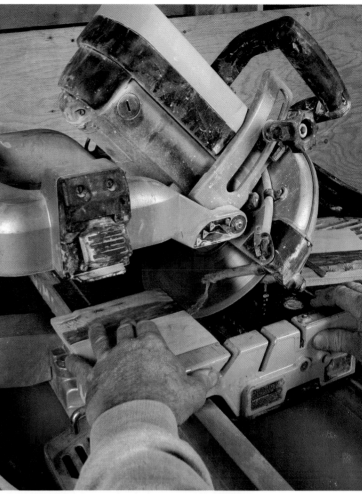

Q The tile wainscot in my bathroom will be capped with a tile chair rail. How do I make the inside and outside miter cuts?

A Although these cuts are 45-degree miters, the easiest way to cut them accurately is with a saw that has a bevel function—basically a tilting head. Unlike modern wood-cutting miter saws, the heads of wet saws tilt only in one direction, so the tile needs to be spun end for end when making matched inside and outside cuts. Again, a large-diameter blade makes it a bit easier to keep your hands firmly positioned during these cuts. This bevel function also comes in handy on scenic tiles such as the ones shown at right, that need to turn a corner without an interruption in the artwork. My two favorite saws for making these cuts are the DeWalt D24000 and the MK TX-3.

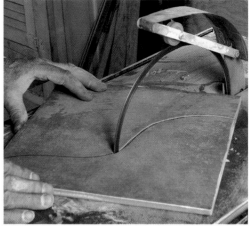

Learning curves. Ring-blade tile saws can make cuts that would be very difficult or impossible with a conventional wet saw. Large tiles such as the one shown at right might need to be cut from both directions.

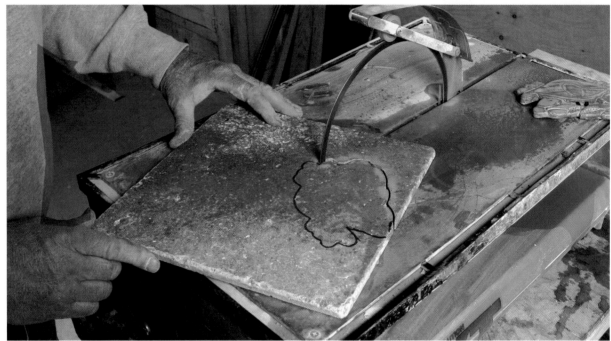

Q I want to do something special by incorporating curves and inlays in my tilework. Can this work be done with a standard wet saw?

A Simple curves can be done with the help of a standard wet saw, a pair of tile nippers, and some quick touch-up with a grinder/polisher. Anything more complicated than that requires a specialized tool called a ring saw, which is a cross between a tile saw and a bandsaw. The advantages of a ring saw are that the cuts are smooth, accurate, and usually accomplished successfully on the first tile, which reduces aggravation and waste.

Q I'm tiling the floor in my kitchen this winter, and I don't want to work outside in the cold. Is a wet saw OK to use indoors?

A Unlike cutting wood inside, dust isn't a concern when cutting tiles, but water is. It's hard to look at a wet saw and judge whether it will keep water contained or drench everything in a 5-ft. radius. Most models have a small rubber flap on the back of the blade hood that is supposed to prevent water from spinning off the blade; I often supplement these flaps with a larger piece of tile membrane (see the left photo above).

The other concern is water running off the edges of the cutting table, particularly a problem when cutting large tiles that hang over the edges. Some wet saws—DeWalt's D24000 and Ridgid's R4010, for instance—have sloped trays to collect overspray and direct it back toward the water reservoir. The trade-off here is a much larger setup. The MK TX-3 (see the right photo above), which uses a misting system, is also a drier alternative.

Noise is also a consideration in confined indoor setups. Tile saws with belt-driven motors run much more quietly than tile saws with direct-drive motors. The Husqvarna TS 250 is an excellent choice.

Q My local home center has compact wet saws that cost about $100. Why should I pay more?

A Whatever you do, don't waste money on a throwaway tile saw. If you choose an inexpensive tile saw made with almost all plastic parts, an underpowered motor, and a cheap water pump, you will be disappointed with the cutting performance. Hard porcelain and granite destroy those weak machines, and a weak machine can destroy fragile marble or glass tile.

If it comes down to price or if you do only a few tile jobs a year, I recommend renting a good tile saw instead. The rental fee is reasonable, eliminates the worry of where to store a tool that is used only occasionally, and allows you to choose the type of saw you rent based on the type of job.

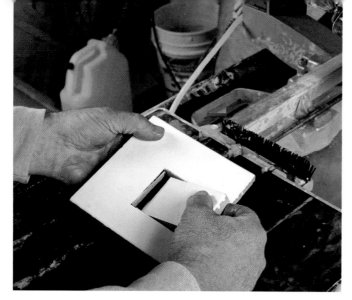

Q I want to finish my kitchen backsplash with 6x6 ceramic tiles. What's a good saw for cutting tiles to fit around electrical outlets and switches?

A Tricky cuts sometimes can be minimized through careful layout, but often, a tile needs to be cut into a U-shaped piece—also referred to as a "pair of pants"—to fit around an electrical box or other obstacle.

In these cases, I often lift the tile into the blade; larger-diameter blades are helpful here. Remember, only half of the blade is exposed, which means you have less than 3½ in. of working room with a 7-in. blade. Larger machines have a 10-in. blade, thus more room for your hands and for the tilted tile. The Husqvarna TS 250 has excellent working room around the blade and is one of the best saws for this task.

If you aren't comfortable lifting the tile into the blade—and to be honest, only a professional should be comfortable doing this—I suggest that you mark the cut on the back side of the tile and cut past the intended line. The curve of the blade will leave you with a clean cut on the front side. Don't worry if it's not perfect; the edges of the cut will be covered by the outlet cover plate.

Tom Meehan is a second-generation tile installer who has been installing tile for more than 35 years. Tom lives with his wife, Lane, and their four sons in Harwich, Massachusetts, where they own Cape Cod Tileworks.

If I Could Have Only One, I'd Pick Two

In some ways, a wet saw is a wet saw. All but the obscure specialty saws use diamond-coated circular sawblades cooled by water that is either held below the blade or pumped from a reservoir.

But of all the saws I've borrowed, bought, or been given, the DeWalt D24000 is my favorite. This is the wet saw that tile installers have been waiting for. Not only does it cut perfect miters in any kind of raised trim pieces, but the 1½-hp motor muscles through heavy-duty straight cuts, too. The saw weighs only 69 lb., and the stand adjusts to four different working heights. A pair of adjustable water nozzles—one on each side of the blade—let me put water where I need it for different cutting tasks. The saw is big, but that's a small price to pay for water overspray guards and collection trays that almost eliminate the need for tarps.

There are times when a large saw is overkill, so I keep an MK-170 in my van, too. It's not on par with saws that have sliding tables, but it's a good ace up my sleeve.

MK Diamond MK-170

DeWalt D24000

Sources

DeWalt
800-4-DEWALT
www.dewalt.com
D24000

Gemini Saw Company
310-891-0288
www.geminisaw.com
Revolution XT tile saw

Husqvarna
913-928-1000
http://us.husqvarnacp.com
Tilematic TS 250

Kraft Tool Co.
800-422-2448
www.krafttool.com
Superior Tile Cutter

MK Diamond Products, Inc.
800-421-5830
www.mkdiamond.com
MK-170, MK-370 and MK TX-3

Ridgid
800-4-RIDGID
www.ridgid.com
R4010

Cutting Ceramic Tile

■ BY DAVID HART

If it weren't for the cutting, tile work would be relatively easy. But tile is both hard and brittle—about as unforgiving as a material can be—and you always need to cut tile during an installation. Luckily, specialized cutting tools and techniques make this job much easier and can keep a potentially beautiful tile job from becoming a mediocre one.

Because the tools are specialized, though, more than one type of cutter is needed to complete all but the most basic installations. I never show up on a job with fewer than three different tile cutters. Also, remember that working with tile is like breaking glass all day long: Safety glasses are a must, and gloves are a good idea.

Cutting Boards: A Basic Straight-Cut Tool

Manual cutting boards are easy to use and cut most common types of ceramic tile. These simple cutters work much like a glass-cutter and use a carbide wheel mounted on a handle to score the tile's ceramic surface. After the tile is scored, the same handle is used to snap the tile along the scored line (see "Using a Cutting Board" on the facing page). I can cut a tile this way in seconds, and I have to set only the cutting board's stop to make repeated cuts.

Cutting boards are available in a variety of models that handle up to 20-in.-wide tiles. I own a smaller board, which cuts tiles up to 10 in., and a larger two-rail model, which has a 20-in. capacity. Both cut tiles on a diagonal, although a wet saw makes those cuts faster and cleaner. The boards don't require more maintenance than an occasional drop or two of oil along the rail and the cutting wheels are replaceable.

Cutting boards have limitations: They cut only straight lines. Sometimes the break can veer from the scored line, resulting in a tile that has to be recut or finished with another tool. Cutting boards also can't cut marble, stone, or thick quarry tile, and they can't take off a thin sliver of tile.

Using a Cutting Board

Under light, even pressure, the cutting wheel scores a line across the tile's surface (see photo at right). The handle is then levered down onto the tile, snapping it along the score (see photo at far right).

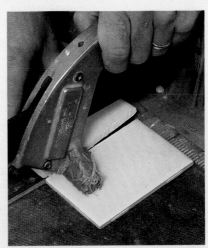

One Tool Won't Do the Job

The tools shown here all cut tile but work best when used together. The cutting boards are portable; the wet saws make the cleanest cuts; and the nippers fit in your pocket and are used to remove waste or to fine-tune a cut.

Wet saw

Cutting board

Nippers

Large-capacity cutting board

Nippers Take Care of the Details

Another essential tile tool is a pair of nippers (see "One Tool Won't Do the Job" at left), sometimes called biters. Nippers are used to break pieces from tile, and as the name suggests, they work best when they take small bites. A common mistake when using nippers is to take too big a bite, which usually cracks the tile in half. Also, instead of crunching through the tile, I've found that nippers work better if you grab the tile and lever down, snapping off the piece.

If a pipe falls on a joint between two tiles, I use nippers to cut an arc in the tile. I also use them to trim off a thin slice from tile that my cutting board can't break (see "Cutting Tile with Nippers," below). Remember to be careful when you use nippers: The tile's cut edges are as sharp as broken glass and can easily slice an unwary hand.

Cutting Tile with Nippers

Cutting boards can score but can't snap a thin offcut, a job perfectly suited to nippers. Grabbing the waste and levering down with the nippers (see the photo at right) usually produces a clean break. Any remainder can be nipped away as needed. When breaking out a small radius (see the photo at far right), it's better to take small, measured bites, especially as you get closer to the line. Large bites tend to crack the tile.

Making a U-Shaped Cut

Tile often must be cut to fit around light switches or soap dishes. Although nippers or a dry saw might work, a wet saw makes the cleanest cut. With the tile held flat on the saw bed, the two parallel cuts are made (photos 1 and 2) by pushing the tile into the blade.

To make the crosscut, many professionals might lift the tile into the blade. However, saw manufacturers recommend that the sawblade be plunged into the tile instead. After loosening the saw head's depth adjustment, you raise the head and turn over the tile. Aligned beneath the blade, the tile is held firmly while the blade is plunged into the cut (photo 3).

Cutting a Radius

To cut around a closet flange, the author makes straight cuts by holding one end of the tile on the bed and carefully lifting the other end into the blade (see the photo below). (Although not sharp, diamond blades should be treated with caution.) The waste is removed at the line with nippers (see the photo at right).

Wet Saws Are Messy but Make the Cleanest Cut

Wet saws are simple to use and versatile. I can cut fairly precise semicircles and other complex shapes with the help of a pair of nippers (see "Making a U-Shaped Cut" on p. 135 and "Cutting a Radius," above). Some cuts aren't easy, and I've gone through three or four pieces of tile before I successfully completed the cut. (That's why it's important to buy extra tile.) I can do some jobs, especially those with small tiles, without a wet saw; but for installations of large, thick, or hard tiles, I have a wet saw ready to go.

The saws typically consist of a 1-hp (or larger) motor mounted over a shallow tub filled with water. The motor powers a diamond blade, usually 8 in. or 10 in. in diameter; a small pump sprays water onto the blade to cool and lubricate it and to keep tile dust to a minimum. The tile sits on a sliding table that rides just above the water on a pair of rails.

To make a cut, I keep the tile flat on the sliding table and push the tile into the spinning blade under even pressure. The best way to make precise cuts is to mark the cut on the face of the tile with a regular pencil or a grease pencil. On dark tiles, I stick masking tape to the tile and mark the tape.

More than a dozen manufacturers make various styles of wet saws (see "Sources" on p. 139). They all cut tile, but I discovered that the smaller tabletop saws just don't perform as well as larger, more expensive models.

I bought a tabletop wet saw when I first started my business and got rid of it two weeks later. It worked well enough, but it lacked a substantial blade guard and threw tile chips and water all over me. If you plan to take on several tile jobs over the course of a few years, it might be worthwhile to buy a larger wet saw.

If you plan to do only one or two jobs, you can rent a wet saw at most tile distributors or home centers. With a little planning, you can do the necessary cutting in a day or two, no matter how large or complicated the job.

Other small wet saws use an angle grinder equipped with a 4-in. or 5-in. blade, a tub of water, and a small rolling tray. Like the first wet saw I bought, these saws work. But they have limitations, and I don't know a single full-time tile contractor who uses one.

No matter what type of wet saw I use, I always set up outside or in an area that can get wet and dirty. I never set up the saw over hardwood flooring (leaks from the saw's water tray stain wood), and I don't use it in a finished house for fear of damaging walls or flooring with the dust and water that inevitably spray from the blade.

Dry-Cutting with Angle Grinders and Diamond Blades

One of the best innovations in the tile industry is a dry-cut diamond blade that fits on an angle grinder (see "Dry-Saw Cutting" on p. 138 and "Cutting Holes with a Dry Saw" on p. 138). Granite, marble, limestone, ceramic, and quarry tile cut as if they were butter with this setup. I use a 4-in. blade on a Makita grinder (see "Sources" on p. 139) that has a fast blade rotation and can make fairly straight cuts, curves, L- and U-shapes and holes in the middle of a tile.

My angle grinder has limitations. It tends to chip the glaze on most ceramic tile and it leaves a rough edge on a piece of marble or granite. I don't use it when that cut edge is to be exposed.

Dry-cut saws are also fairly dangerous if they aren't used properly. Because the grinder has a tendency to jump when it starts to cut, it's important to hold tightly onto this tool.

Tape Tip

Forget a white pencil? When you're marking dark tiles, a pencil line drawn on a piece of tape becomes a good substitute for a grease pencil or a crayon. The mark can be full length on the tile or just serve as a crow's foot.

Dry-Saw Cutting

An angle grinder fitted with a diamond blade makes quick work of freehand tile cuts, but this tool is noisy, throws lots of dust, and should be used outside with a dust mask. To cut a radius, the author firmly secures the tile with one hand, and holding the grinder in a tight grip throughout the process, he makes a series of shallow, scoring cuts along the pencil line. The shallow cuts keep the blade from binding in the material; as the blade progresses down into the material, the kerf should be widened toward the waste to allow the blade easier passage.

Cutting Holes with a Dry Saw

Bathtub plumbing often exits the wall in the middle of a tile. If a hole saw isn't handy, the next best thing is a dry saw. The angle grinder offers a quick, if rough, way of cutting a hole in the middle of a tile.

After measuring a square that's large enough to fit around the pipe but small enough to be covered by the flange, the author marks the tile on both sides and makes four small plunge cuts into the back of the tile (see the large photo at right). The front of the tile must be checked periodically to make sure the cuts don't go beyond the lines (see the small photo at right).

When the cuts on the back have extended nearly to the corners drawn on the front, the tile is flipped, and the cuts can be finished from the front.

Grinders are equipped with a blade guard that some tile installers remove. I've always kept on the blade guard, and on a couple of occasions when the tool kicked back and hit me in the leg, the blade guard probably saved me from a trip to the hospital.

These tools also throw clouds of dust, so I use them outside unless the situation requires indoor use. For instance, I've used my grinder to cut installed tile to retrofit electrical outlets, floor vents, and even plumbing fixtures. When I cut indoors, I have an assistant hold a vacuum cleaner behind the blade to suck up the huge amount of dust that accompanies these tools. A vacuum won't get it all, however, so I cover anything that needs to stay dust-free.

Angle grinders are standard tools among professional tile installers, and anyone who plans to do several installations should consider purchasing one.

Hole Saws for a Perfect Circle

If I want to cut a hole in the middle of a tile for a plumbing-supply line, I sometimes use a hole saw (see "Cutting the Perfect Hole" below). These tools have a carbide or diamond-tipped pilot bit and a diamond-edged hole saw, and they can cut through a soft-bodied ceramic or marble tile in less than a minute.

However, they don't work well on extremely hard ceramic tiles, marble or granite unless you use a hammer drill, and even that doesn't always cut through the hardest tiles. Hole saws come in several sizes; I own a 1¼-in.-dia. model and use a dry-cut grinder for larger holes.

David Hart is a tile contractor and outdoors writer living in Rice, Virginia.

Sources

Below is a partial list of tile-saw, blade, and tool manufacturers. A number of tool-supply houses on the Web carry a wide selection of tile tools.

Crain Tools
408-946-6100
www.craintools.com

Husqvarna
913-928-1000
http://us.husqvarnacp.com

Makita
800-462-5482
www.makita.com

MK Diamond Products, Inc.
800-421-5830
www.mkdiamond.com

Q.E.P. Co. Inc.
866-435-8665
www.qep.com

Rubi Tools USA Inc.
866-USA-RUBI
www.rubi.com

Cutting the Perfect Hole

A diamond-coated hole saw chucked into a ⅜-in. drill cuts a clean hole in most ceramic tiles. Available in different diameters, hole saws are a bit slower cutting than dry saws. They also can't cut harder tiles or granite as easily but are still a good choice for production work.

Grouting Tile

■ BY DAVID HART

If there's one thing that most tile install-ers dislike, it's grouting. A monotonous, shoulder-wrenching task, grouting is often delegated to the low man on the totem pole. That's a big mistake. Nothing can ruin a top-notch tile installation quicker than a bad grout job. An inexperienced helper can leave shaded or splotchy grout, uneven joints, or grout that can be scratched out of a joint with the stroke of a fingernail.

Years ago, white-wall grout was nothing more than portland cement mixed with water; floor grout was mixed on the job by combining fine white sand with cement in a 1:1 ratio. Latex or polymer additives weren't an option, so installers simply added water to the mix. It worked—tile that was installed 50 or more years ago remains intact in many homes—but it had its limitations. Color choices were usually limited to white, black, or gray. These days, grout is available in a rainbow of colors.

Modern grout products are also stronger and easier to use. The only factors that need concern tile installers are the type of grout to use, the proper consistency of the mix, even application, and a thorough cleaning. And they shouldn't forget additives and sealants.

Epoxy Grout Is Not for Everyone

Epoxy grout is the most stain-resistant grout you can find, which makes it a great choice for use on kitchen counters and in res-taurants and medical facilities.

It is, however, an unforgiving material to work. It's sold as a two-part additive that's mixed with regular grout or as a two-part ready mix that can also be used as a setting compound; either way, you have to mix the entire batch at one time to maintain proper propor-tions. There's no mixing by eye. It can be used only with ceramic tile and can't be removed from a porous surface.

Cleaning is often a frustrating experience that involves removing excess grout with nylon scrub pads and lots of water (epoxy isn't water soluble). Here, timing is really important. If you clean before the grout has set, the sticky epoxy pulls out of the joints and smears all over; wait a few minutes too long, and you'll be hard-pressed to remove it with a hammer and chisel.

If this material were just difficult and expensive, I still might use it, but most regular grouts now include latex additives far superior to their counterparts of the past. Coupled with a good sealer, these newer fortified grouts are stain resistant and hold up well under normal household abuse. Given the extra expense, time, and elbow grease required by epoxy mixes, I can't think of a good reason to use epoxy unless a customer requests it. I certainly wouldn't recommend it to any neophyte tilesetters. (For another opinion on epoxy grout, see "A Fearless Approach to Epoxy Grout" on p. 148.)

The Width of the Joint Determines the Type of Grout

There are two basic types of grout: sanded and unsanded. Which one you use is usually determined by the width of the joint be-tween the tiles. Unsanded grout is the prod-uct of choice for any tile installation where the joints are less than ⅛ in. wide, even on floor tile. The finish is smooth, and it is rela-tively easy to clean.

Primarily used in joints wider than ⅛ in., sanded grout (also called floor grout or joint filler) provides the necessary strength for joints up to ½ in. and even wider. Although you might get away with unsanded grout in joints slightly wider than ⅛ in., it's a poor bet. More than likely, tiny hairline cracks

will form as a result of shrinkage, which is controlled by sand in the mixture.

As you might guess, the texture of sanded grout is rougher and a bit harder to clean. Although sanded grout is associated primar-ily with floor tile, it should be used on any tile with wider joints, no matter where it's installed. However, be prepared for a long day if you plan to grout a wall with sanded grout. Unsanded grout readily clings to ver-tical surfaces, but sanded grout tends to roll down the wall and end up in little piles on the floor. It's possible to use sanded grout in thin joints, too, but pushing the thicker mixture into tight grout joints can be a frus-trating task that typically leaves small pin-holes in the grout finish.

Unlike products of 10 years ago, most grouts on the market now include a latex

Careful mixing controls the ratio of water to powder. Mixing grout is often a process of estimating by eye; water should be added gradually to the powder to achieve the right mix. Clean water and a clean bucket are important ingredients.

Proper consistency ensures long-lasting grout. It's important that the final mix have a stiff, toothpaste-like texture that's easy to work into joints. Too much water weakens the grout and makes it runny; too little water makes it set up too fast.

or polymer additive that strengthens the grout and helps it resist staining. Although you can buy grout without admixes, I don't bother; I'd rather have the extra protection that admixes offer.

To determine the amount of grout you will need to buy, consult the chart on the back of every bag of grout, or ask the sales clerk at the tile distributor. Measurements are typically based on the square-foot coverage per pound of grout, so you need to know how many square feet the job is, how wide the joints are, and how big the tile is. One pound of grout might cover 5 sq. ft. of 6-in. by 6-in. tile with ¼-in. joints; a 25-lb. bag of grout typically covers about 100 sq. ft. of 8-in. by 8-in. tile with ¼-in. joints. I've used a half-dozen different brands, and all seemed to work well; none stood out as inferior or difficult to work.

Successful Grouting Depends on the Right Consistency

One of the most important aspects of grout is the mix. Nothing can make the process of spreading grout more difficult than adding too little water to the powder. A stiff grout mixture can be nearly impossible to push across the tile and into the joints. Conversely, nothing can ruin grout faster than adding too much water.

I generally mix grout by hand with a margin trowel (see "Essential Grouting Tools" on the facing page) in a clean 5-gal. bucket (see the right photo above). When I need a large amount, I save time by mixing with a paddle bit chucked into a variable-speed drill. A word of caution here: Whipping the grout

Essential Grouting Tools

Floats: You can't grout without a float. They're available in two varieties: floor floats and wall floats. Wall floats have a soft rubber pad, while floor floats are much stiffer. Although some contractors use both, I use a wall float for all my grouting; I've found that a floor float is too inflexible to get into tight corners. A good-quality float should last up to a year for a full-time installer. Eventually, the edges of the float wear down and won't clean off the face of the tile well.

Margin Trowel: This spatula-shaped tool is essential for mixing grout and for scraping it out of corners and along baseboards. It's also good for cleaning your other tools at the end of the day. A typical margin trowel will last for several years.

Sponges: A good-quality grout sponge is an essential tool for which there is no cheap substitute. I always use large grout sponges because they pick up and hold more grout than smaller ones, and that saves time.

Gloves: Although some tile installers never wear rubber gloves when grouting, I won't grout without them. I don't like to have wrinkled skin at the end of a long day and, inevitably, the dry, rough skin that follows. Frankly, there's no reason not to wear long rubber gloves. Although I have used grocery-store gloves, they're too thin and rip far too easily. I use a pair of heavy gloves sold at tile distributors that have lasted almost a year.

Kneepads: If you plan to spend more than an hour on your knees on a tile floor, you need kneepads. It's foolish to work without them. You can find a cheap pair but you get what you pay for. I have a pair of plastic-capped, foam-lined kneepads from Alta® (see "Sources" on p. 147) and they still protect me after three years of hard use.

---

into a froth can create air bubbles that will weaken the mix, so go slowly.

Generally, less water is better. As the water evaporates from a typical mix, it leaves microscopic voids. Excess water takes up more space; when the water evaporates, it creates larger voids and weak grout.

What's the right water-to-grout ratio? Most contractors (me included) eyeball the right balance between powder and water. Grout manufacturers usually recommend a ratio when mixing a whole bag ("mix 25 lb. of grout with 3½ qt. to 4 qt. of clean water," for instance). But there are times when you won't use that much, so you have to estimate. I always add less water than I think I need, and then add a little more if necessary.

Both sanded and unsanded grouts should have a stiff, toothpaste-like consistency when completely blended (see the left photo on the facing page). The mix should be allowed to sit for about 10 minutes and then

be mixed again, an important step called slaking. Slaking allows the ingredients to react and the color pigments to blend, creating a stronger grout with uniform color.

Working the Grout into Place

Once I've mixed the grout a second time, I dump a pile of it onto the floor and start pushing it around with a float held up at about a 45-degree angle (see the top drawing on the facing page). I want to make sure the joints are full, so I bear down on the float as I sweep it diagonally across the joints.

I grout a small area, as much as I can reach easily, then go back and pull the float hard diagonally across the tile, holding the float at almost a 90-degree angle. This step cleans off the large chunks of grout left behind and helps facilitate a quick cleanup later.

When I'm grouting walls, I usually load up a float with wall grout, start at the bot-

tom and spread it up the wall (see the left photo above), leaving plenty of grout on the face of the tile. I go back and clean off the excess grout by holding the float at a sharp angle and pulling it across the tile on a diagonal (see the right photo above). As before, I push down on the float pretty hard as I pull it across the tile.

In average conditions, grout begins to set up in about 30 minutes, so I try not to spread more than I can work with in that time. If I'm working in hot rooms or with porous tile, I spread just enough so that I can start the initial cleanup in 15 minutes to 30 minutes. I've also found that grout will set faster if left in the bucket, so I dump the entire mix onto the floor and keep it moving until it's gone.

Although cold joints aren't an issue with grout, there is a chance of color variation from one batch to the next. If I have to stop, I try to end at a doorway or clear delineation and feather the next day's work over the old.

The Trick Is to Work One Area at a Time

Working within arm's reach, the author packs grout into the tile joints with broad sweeps across the tile face. Working diagonally on subsequent passes pushes the excess grout to the next area.

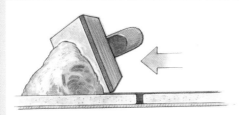

Keep the float at an angle. To pack grout into joints, apply steady pressure with the float held at an approximately 45-degree angle. A second pass with the float held closer to 90 degrees will clean excess grout from the tile.

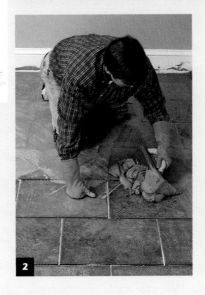

Where Not to Grout

Grout won't crack between wall tiles that are properly installed, except at the junction of the tile and an abutting structure like a tub or a countertop. If I'm working with large tiles, I try to minimize the amount of grout I pack into these expansion joints. Otherwise, I grout everything, use a margin trowel or utility knife to cut out the grout before it hardens, and then run a bead of latex-silicone caulk into the joint. Latex-silicone is easy to use and easy to clean up. Although it doesn't last as long as a pure silicone caulk, it does a fine job of protecting against water damage.

If you're concerned about matching that mauve or orange grout, most manufacturers now sell caulks that are color-matched to their grouts.

A clean sponge picks up more grout. When the sponge's pores begin to clog with grout, the sponge should be rinsed and squeezed nearly dry. Excess water left standing on the joints will affect the curing process and discolor the grout.

Cleanup starts with lots of sponge and little water. Once grout has firmed up in the joints, it's important to clean the tile and smooth the joints before the grout hardens. A damp sponge will clean up the majority of the grout.

Final Cleanup Needs Less Water

Cleaning up is as important as choosing and mixing the grout. The initial cleanup should accomplish two things: First, it should remove the bulk of the residual grout on the face of the tile; and second, it should smooth the joints without pulling out the grout.

When the grout in the joints has firmed up to where it isn't soft to the touch, I start cleaning. How long should firming up take? It varies with room temperature, humidity, and the amount of water used in the mixture, but generally, it takes 15 to 30 minutes. If I wait too long, the grout will dry on the face of the tile, and I'll have to scrape it off. In hot weather or direct sunlight, grout can stick to tile within 15 minutes.

I start with two buckets of clean water, a couple of large sponges, a margin trowel, and a grout float. After wetting a sponge and wringing it out, I wipe the face of the tile and the joints with a light circular motion (see the photos above), rinsing the sponge when the pores become clogged with grout. If the grout is pulling out of the joints, I wait a few more minutes. During this pass, I want to loosen the grout that's drying on the tile. To avoid splotchy color, I also make sure I don't leave puddles of water on the joints. I use a margin trowel to scrape clumps of grout out of the corners, door casings, and any other place where it doesn't belong.

After I've smoothed the joints and loosened the grout stuck to the tile face, I go back with a bucket of clean water and remove the light grout haze that remains. With a clean, lightly dampened sponge, I wipe diagonally across the tile (see the photo on the facing page) for about 2 ft. or 3 ft., taking care not to push down too hard. I then turn over the sponge, repeat, and rinse the sponge. This process takes time, and if I rush it, I end up smearing grout across the tile. Any streaks of grout haze left after the second wipe-down can be removed with a damp rag or mop when the grout has dried.

Second cleaning removes the grout haze. After the initial cleaning, the remaining grout residue can be wiped up with a clean, damp sponge and light strokes. It's important to rinse the sponge frequently during this stage.

Cleaning and Sealing Tile

Clients often tell me they want a maintenance-free floor, but there really is no such thing, at least not with tile, stone, or marble. There is no substitute for general maintenance and upkeep; grout gets dirty, period. It's important to clean grout on a regular basis with a plastic-bristle brush and a commercial grout cleaner or a solution of mild soap and water. Make sure the soap isn't oil-based; products such as Pine-Sol® and Murphy® Oil Soap will darken the grout.

Sealers offer a way of protecting grout from stains; I usually recommend a sealer on floor installations. After trying several formulas available, I've found that the easiest to use is a water-based penetrating sealer such as TEC™ silicone sealer or TileLab® Grout & Tile Sealer (see "Sources" at right), which soaks into the grout and then dries without changing the appearance. (Sealer manufacturers recommend different waiting periods before sealer application, so consult the product literature first.)

No matter what type of sealer I use, it's often necessary to apply a fresh coat at least once a year, sometimes more often. After first cleaning the grout joints, I paint the sealer onto the joint with a foam or bristle brush, allow a few minutes for it to soak in, and then wipe off any remaining liquid. I try not to let the sealer dry on the face of the tile, but if the sealer does dry, a quick scrub with a mild abrasive cleaner removes it. After I apply the first coat, I try applying a second coat, but often it won't soak in. That's okay; it simply means the grout is properly sealed. If the second coat does soak in (the grout will turn dark as it would if it were wet), I simply continue with the rest of the wall or floor.

Other types of sealers include acrylic-based topcoats that leave a shiny film on the surface of the grout and oil-based sealers that will permanently darken the color of the grout. They all work, but each variety leaves a different finish on the grout. Just test the sealers in a hidden area first.

David Hart is a tile contractor and outdoors writer living in Rice, Virginia.

Sources

Alta
800-788-0302
www.altaindustries.com

Custom Building Products
800-272-8786
www.custombuildingproducts.com
TileLab Grout & Tile Sealer

TEC
800-TEC-9002
www.tecspecialty.com
TEC silicone sealer

A Fearless Approach to Epoxy Grout

■ BY TOM MEEHAN

For the past 25 years, tilesetters have been relying on epoxy grout as their ace in the hole for grouting stain-prone areas such as countertops, showers, and high-traffic bathroom floors. The early forms of epoxy grout quickly earned the material a reputation for being difficult and messy. I can attest to that fact, too. Epoxy grout used to be tricky to mix and difficult to spread, and the smell always left me feeling sick by day's end. Unless the mixture was perfect, the temperature was fixed, and the moon was in alignment with Saturn and Pluto, the goopy grout would sag in wall joints and settle below the edges of floor tiles. The cleanup, which was unforgiving in every sense of the word, often concluded with my work clothes being tossed in the garbage. If you can approach the material with an open mind, though, I think you will find that today's epoxy-grout products have changed for the better.

Several manufacturers make epoxy grout (see "Sources" on p. 151), and although their products differ slightly, all have significantly

I use Laticrete's SpectraLock® Pro epoxy grout (see "Sources" on p. 151). The kit shown at far right includes most of the materials you need for a smooth installation. Part C (see the photo at near right), which adds color, is sold separately. If you choose another brand, make sure to have these essentials.

Bucket

If the epoxy-grout kit doesn't come in a bucket, you will need one. Be sure to wash out remaining grout before using the bucket for cleanup.

Float

Some manufacturers offer special epoxy-grout floats, which are made from a harder rubber. I've found that a premium-quality traditional float (a new one, preferably) is a fine substitute.

Gloves

Epoxy chemicals aren't just messy. They also can irritate your skin. Kits include thin latex gloves, but I prefer slightly thicker grouting gloves.

Mixing tools

I use a margin trowel for mixing small batches of grout, but if the job requires a large portion, I use a drill-powered paddle mixer. Clean tools right after mixing.

Rags

Avoid materials such as terry cloth towels that could leave fuzz in the grout joints; a clean cotton cloth is the best bet.

Sponge

Don't risk being left with yellow sponge crumbs in cured grout joints. Use a new sponge for every installation.

---

simplified the installation process. The Laticrete product I use is sold in kits, which include individually measured components that ensure the right mix every time. A pair of gloves in each bucket guards against the temptation to work unprotected, packaged additives make cleanup easier, and a fresh sponge means less chance of leaving yellow bits of debris in cured joints. If you throw in your own grout float and heed the advice offered here, a smooth installation is in the bag.

Epoxy Grout Needs a Well-Prepped Surface

Once you've assembled your kit (see the sidebar above) and have the necessary supplies close at hand, there are a few housekeeping items to check off the list before mixing the epoxy components.

First you need to clean the joints. Use a utility knife or the edge of a margin trowel to remove any hardened chunks of thinset

TIP

Do a small job or sample area with epoxy before tackling the important job. Like anything new, epoxy just takes a little time to get used to.

Clean the joints.

Seal the tile.

Part A

Part B

Part C

from the tile. Nothing in the joints should be within ⅛ in. of the tile surface.

Next, vacuum the joint. This step is often skipped, but it's a must. Any dust or small specks of debris left on the floor will appear in the grout joints. The tacky epoxy makes debris difficult to remove before it hardens.

After all the debris has been removed from the joints, seal the tile. This is especially important when grouting natural stone (two coats if the stone is extremely porous), but is also a good idea for porcelain and ceramic tile with a flat finish. Allow the sealer to dry for at least a couple of hours.

Lastly, protect the area. Don't risk getting this stuff on your bathroom vanity, baseboard trim, door threshold, carpet, or hardwood flooring. Anything that's near the tile but is not supposed to be grouted should be masked off with painter's tape.

Once You're Mixing, the Clock is Ticking

Expect to have about 80 minutes of working time, but don't try to beat the clock by making only partial batches of grout. If the A:B:C ratio isn't exact, the product won't perform as expected.

Combine Part A and Part B in a clean (preferably new) bucket, mixing with a margin trowel and rolling each bag like a tube

of toothpaste to squeeze out as much liquid as possible. After stirring, add Part C, the cement-based colorant. Blend all three components until the mixture has a consistency similar to sticky cake batter.

Spread Quickly, and Clean Completely

The grouting process for epoxy is basically the same as with conventional grout—pack the joints firmly, but leave as little excess as possible—only the stakes are a bit higher. Work quickly and thoroughly; recklessness will leave you with a mess.

Use the margin trowel to scoop a small pile of grout onto the floor, and begin spreading it across the tile, holding the float at a 30-degree angle to the floor. Once the grout is pushed firmly into the joints, scrape off the excess, holding the float at a 60-degree angle to the floor. Be careful not to dig into the side of the joints, or you'll remove the grout.

The floor should be ready to wash after about 15 to 20 minutes; much longer than that, and the epoxy begins to harden. Make sure to wring out the sponge thoroughly before scrubbing. Too much water dilutes the epoxy, making it weak and discolored.

After both washes have been completed, use a cotton rag to wipe off the remaining

Tile Grout: Epoxy vs. Cement

Laticrete
Spectra Lock

Epoxy grout is expensive but more durable

Epoxy grout has several appealing qualities, including its strength, its stain- and chemical-resistance, and its availability in a broad range of colors. These qualities make it the best choice for heavily trafficked locations or in areas that often come in contact with powerful cleaning agents.

Epoxy grout is applied the same way as cement grout. It's spread over tile with a float and packed into the grout joints. Excess grout is then removed. Although this technique is the same for both types of grout, the stress level is much higher when working with epoxy. This is because epoxy has a shorter working time than cement, especially in warmer temperatures. Also, hardened epoxy is hard to remove, so it's crucial to remove residue completely. Any epoxy left on the tile surface for an extended length of time will likely become a permanent feature.

Another epoxy-grout shortcoming is the possibility of its color darkening or yellowing under exposure to the sun, although that is less likely to occur with new epoxy-grout formulas.

Portland-cement grout is cheap and easy to work with

Sold as a dry mixture, cement-based grout is suitable for most applications. It's readily available in a variety of colors and is more forgiving to work with than epoxy grout. Unlike epoxy grout, its residue can be buffed off tile the day after it's applied.

However, epoxy-grout ingredients are packaged to ensure accurate mixing. Cement grout can be mixed incorrectly if too much or too little water is added, possibly weakening the grout while also causing color to fade or to be inconsistent.

Also, cement-grouted joints require grout sealer, but epoxy-grouted joints don't.

Custom Building
Products Polyblend

Scoop, spread, and scrape the grout across the floor.

Don't wait too long to wash.

Sources

Bostik
800-7BOSTIK
www.bostik-us.com
EzPoxy™ and
Hydroment

**Custom Building
Products**
800-272-8786
www.custombuilding
products.com
Polyblend

**Laticrete
International Inc.**
800-243-4788
www.laticrete.com
SpectraLock Pro

MAPEI
800-426-2734
www.mapei.us

Buff away the haze.

haze. Avoid pushing down too hard with the rag; buff the surface firmly, as if you were waxing a car. Don't stop wiping the surface until every bit of sticky residue is removed. If you are working your way out of the room, make sure to watch out for footprints left on the tile surface.

Tom Meehan is a second-generation tile installer who has been installing tile for more than 35 years. Tom lives with his wife, Lane, and their four sons in Harwich, Massachusetts, where they own Cape Cod Tileworks.

A New Way to Tile a Big Floor

■ BY TOM MEEHAN

There are buildings in Europe with tile floors that are in perfect shape after more than 1,000 years. However, on this side of the pond, tile floors routinely fail after less than 10 years. What did the Europeans of the first millennium know about tile that we have yet to learn?

New Material for an Old System

The answer is that Europeans developed what is known as an uncoupling system. The system began with a bottom layer of mortar covered by a thin layer of sand. The tile then was set into another layer of mortar on top of the sand. As the building settled and shifted over the years, the sand separated the tile from the floor below, allowing the tile to float on top, unaffected by the building's movement.

Without an uncoupling system, the tile floors of today move when the building moves. Results can include loose grout, loose tile, and in extreme cases, cracked tile as the floor surface under the tile moves and shifts, especially if the floor is big.

In the past, I've had pretty good luck by first making sure that the subfloor was thick enough, then applying felt paper, wire lath, and a layer of mortar before installing the tile. But that was a lot of extra work, extra materials, and extra thickness being added to the tile floor. Recently, I started using a product from the Schlüter Company called Ditra, (see "Sources" on p. 162) which applies ancient European concepts using some 21st-century materials (see the sidebar below).

Both Sides of an Uncoupling Membrane

Ditra, made by the Schlüter Company (see "Sources" on p. 162), is an uncoupling membrane that allows the finished floor surface (tile, thinset, and grout) and the substrate (floor sheathing or a floor slab) to move independently of each other. A close look at Ditra reveals the way it works. A fabric backing on one side bonds to the floor, and a keyed plastic grid system on the other side bonds to the tile. When the floor moves, the fabric allows the plastic sheet above it to move without breaking the bond of the tile.

Ditra cuts easily with scissors or a utility knife, and it can be pieced into smaller areas without losing effectiveness.

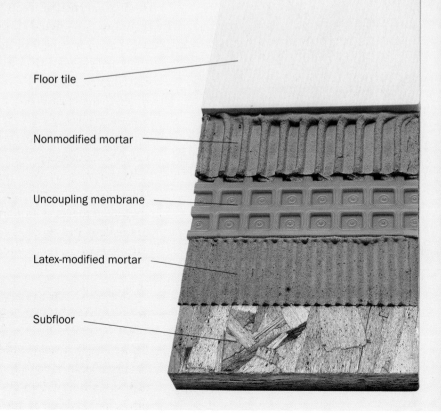

Floor tile

Nonmodified mortar

Uncoupling membrane

Latex-modified mortar

Subfloor

Is Your Floor Strong Enough for Tile?

The Tile Council of America's (see "Sources" on p. 162) standard formula for measuring maximum deflection under a tile floor is called L-360. Divide the total span of the floor joists by 360 for the maximum amount the floor can give in the middle under a live load of 40 lb./sq. ft., plus any long-term deflection due to the weight of the floor.

For example, the maximum allow-able deflection for a joist span of 15 ft. is ½ in. The L-360 standard applies to most ceramic, porcelain, and hard stone. But for certain soft-stone tile, such as limestone or light marble, the L-720 formula applies, cutting the maximum allowable deflection in half.

Ways of reducing deflection include adding extra layers of plywood underlayment or installing additional support under the floor framing.

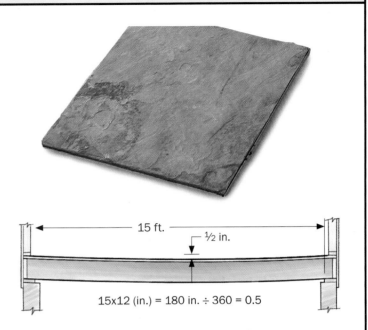

15 ft.

½ in.

15x12 (in.) = 180 in. ÷ 360 = 0.5

Start with a Sound Floor

Adding a membrane under the tile may be a great way to lengthen the life of a tile installation, but the floor below has to be structurally sound. There are formulas for determining if a floor has too much deflection (see the sidebar above), but I've also learned to rely on feel. Too much give when I jump on the floor tells me that it probably needs strengthening.

Whenever possible, I check the framing below the floor to make sure the size and spacing of the joists are correct for the span of the floor. I've even been known to add extra support columns under bouncy floors.

The Membrane Goes Down Quickly

Before I begin installing tile, I roll out and cut pieces of membrane for the whole floor (see photo 1 on p. 156). It's OK to use small pieces in areas such as thresholds to make

Fabric backing

Plastic grid system

Spread out the Membrane

1

Test-fit first. Cut membrane to fit the floor with scissors or a utility knife. Cover the subfloor completely.

2

One course at a time. Spread only enough mortar for one course of membrane, then roll out the pre-cut pieces.

the installation easier. If I'm putting down a heat mat for a radiant floor, I install it before the membrane. The membrane helps to distribute heat from the mat, and it protects the mat if a tile ever needs to be replaced.

I snap chalklines for each course of tile before it's installed to help guide me so that I don't spread more thinset mortar than necessary. For an installation over a wood subfloor, I use a latex-modified thinset that bonds well to the fabric side of the membrane. I start with a skim coat of thinset, pushing it into the pores of the wood with the straight edge of the trowel. Right away, I spread a second layer of mortar with a ³⁄₁₆-in. by ¼-in. V-notched trowel.

I keep the trowel lines going in one direction so that pockets or voids don't form,

which could prevent the membrane from bonding properly. Then I roll the membrane into the fresh mortar and push it out flat (see photo 2 above). Once the membrane is in position, I use either a 75-lb. linoleum roller or a wooden float to press it into the mortar and establish the bond (see photo 3 on the facing page). Push out any excess thinset that may make the floor uneven.

3

Make a good impression. After the membrane is rolled out flat, a wooden float ensures a good bond with the mortar.

Plan Tile Layout for Best Look and Least Waste

Once the first tile goes down, there's no turning back, so I take as much time as I need to get the layout right (see the drawing and photos on pp. 158–159). This floor tile is 12x12 Turkish slate. It varies slightly in size and thickness, and has an uneven cleft face.

In this room, the focal point is the sliding door, so I began my layout there by measuring three courses from that wall and snapping a chalkline across the room. Next, I dry-fit a row of tiles in front of the door to see what cuts I'd end up with beside the slider and at the two sidewalls. I found that centering

the tile on the middle of the door left 11-in. pieces on both sides of the room for minimal waste. Before lifting the tiles in front of the door, I marked the center tile's edge.

Once I have the line across the room and the line for the center course of tile, I project a perpendicular line down the middle of the room (see photo 4 on p. 159) with a straight-edge and a 3-4-5 aSquare® (see "Sources" on p. 162). Measuring off the sidewalls, I extend the centerline to the other end of the room and snap a chalkline. I confirm that the line is perpendicular to the first line between the sidewalls, and when I'm satisfied, I trace over the chalkline with a waterproof marker.

As a final check, I lay out one course of tile along both perpendicular lines without mortar. As I pick up the tile, I mark every three courses and snap parallel chalklines at each mark to keep the courses running straight and true.

Tile Locks into Membrane

I install the tiles over the Ditra using a dry-set thinset mortar instead of latex-modified thinset. Dry-set, or nonmodified, mortar is easier to work with, is easier to clean up, and is about one-third the price of good latex-modified thinset mortar.

Because the slate is uneven and has voids in its surface, I spread the thinset with a coarse ⅜-in. square-notched trowel. Before I comb it with the notched side of the trowel, I push the thinset with the straight edge of the trowel to key it into the recessed dovetailed edges of each square in the membrane. Then I go back over the thinset with the notched side of the trowel, again keeping the lines moving in just one direction.

The first tile determines the position of every tile in the floor, so I set it at the point where the two layout lines intersect (see the center photo on p. 160). As I work down the floor, I apply thinset to an area in which I can set tile within about 15 minutes, usually about 30 sq. ft. at a time. For each set of

Tiling Starts with Careful Layout

Dry-fitting a couple of tile courses enables you to determine the best layout and mark up the floor with layout lines.

1. After tiles are dry-fit in front of the door, measuring the width of the room determines whether the layout should be centered on a tile or on a grout joint for the best use of materials.

2. Mark the edge of the center tile course.

3. Measure three tile courses off the wall, and snap a chalkline across the room.

4. After marking the edge of the center tile, use a large folding square and a straightedge to extend the layout into the room. Measurements to the wall guide the center course line to the other end of the room. Straightedges confirm that the layout lines are perpendicular to each other.

5. A dry course of tile on top of the membrane confirms the side-to-side layout, and another course along the center course line sets the installation spacing every three courses.

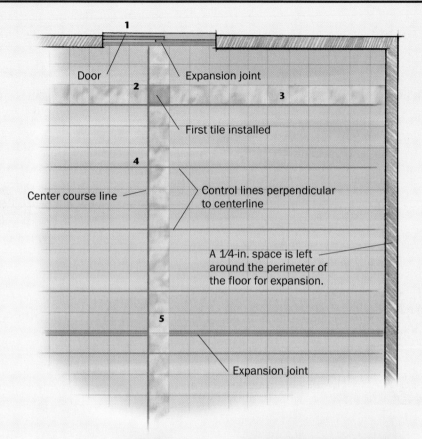

Door

Expansion joint

First tile installed

Center course line

Control lines perpendicular to centerline

A 1/4-in. space is left around the perimeter of the floor for expansion.

Expansion joint

Expansion Joints Let a Big Floor Flex

Expansion joints, recommended every 20 ft. to 24 ft. or wherever tile butts against a wall surface, such as in front of a sliding door, allow the tile to expand and contract with changes in temperature.

1. An L-shaped joint goes against the door. After caulking the edge of the joint with silicone, press it into the mortar and against the door.

2. The first tile set at the intersection of the layout lines establishes the position of every tile in the room.

3. A T-shaped expansion joint goes between tile courses. First, position the joint, then apply a thin layer of mortar over the flanges to keep the joint in place while you set the tile.

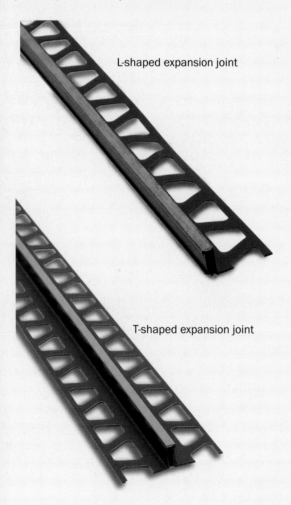

L-shaped expansion joint

T-shaped expansion joint

Seal, Grout, Then Seal Again

Sealing stone tile before grouting helps to keep the grout from sticking and makes cleanup easier.

1. Applying the first coat of sealer with a rag keeps it from going into open grout joints.

2. The author pushes a large volume of grout to make sure it is packed deep into all the joints.

3. To bridge the uneven edges between the stone tiles, a gloved palm shapes the grout into a bevel.

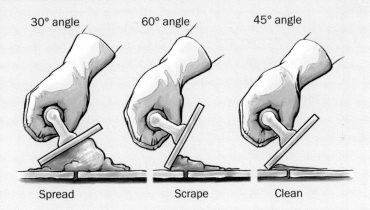

30° angle   60° angle   45° angle

Spread   Scrape   Clean

4. The second coat of sealer seals the grout and adds extra protection to the stone tile.

1

2

3

4

courses, I install the first tile at the intersection of the layout lines. As each tile goes in, I apply a little downward pressure and slide the tile into place, which helps to lock the tile into the layer of thinset.

Because these tiles vary in thickness, I butter the backs of thinner tiles with a little thinset to bring them to the height of the other tiles. If a tile is extremely irregular in either shape or thickness, I put it aside for cuts or to be used in a closet.

As with most stone tile, each piece varies in shade and color. To keep color variations consistent across the floor, I work with tile from several boxes at a time. If a tile happens to have a color that is too extreme, I set it aside.

Expansion Joints Give Tile Extra Breathing Room

In large floors, expansion joints should be installed every 20 ft. to 24 ft. Without expansion joints, there's an increased risk of cracks as the tile expands and contracts due to temperature changes.

The expansion joints I use (also made by the Schlüter Company) are available L-shaped for along walls, or T-shaped for between tile courses (see the photos on p. 160). A section of L-shaped expansion joint was needed in front of the sliding doors, where it also helps to prevent the tile and grout from cracking as the door is opened and closed repeatedly.

Because this room is just over 24 ft. long, I put a T-shaped expansion joint between two courses roughly in the middle of the room. Once I determine where the joint will be, I press it into the thinset, measuring to keep the joint at the right distance from the previous course. I trowel a little thinset over the flange before setting the tile.

I like to lay tile before baseboard goes in, so I leave a ¼-in. expansion gap along the walls for seasonal tile movement. The base-

board will hide the gap when it's installed. If the base is in before I tile, I can put L-shaped expansion joints around the perimeter of the floor.

Seal Tile Before You Grout

After all the tile is in, but before it's grouted, I give the floor a thorough cleaning. I not only wash the surface of the tile, but I also remove any thinset that is too high in the joints between the tiles. The thinset should be at least ⅛ in. below the surface of the tile.

After the tile is clean, I wipe the first of two coats of sealer onto the tile with a rag to avoid getting sealer into joints (see the photos on p. 161). I prefer Miracle Sealants' Porous Plus (see "Sources" at left). Because slate is porous and has an irregular surface, the sealer makes cleaning off grout easier.

To spread the grout and push it deep into the joints, I begin with the grout trowel at a 30-degree angle (see the drawing on p. 161). Next, I scrape the residue off the tiles with the trowel at a 60-degree angle. Finally, I remove excess grout by dragging the trowel across the tiles and joints at a 45-degree angle to avoid pulling the grout out of the joints. Because of the uneven edges of the slate tile, I use the palm of my hand to bevel the grout between tiles as I spread it.

After the grout has set up, I wipe down the tile with terry cloth to remove grout crumbs. Then I clean the tile with cool, clean water and a sponge. Cleaning requires extra diligence to remove all the grout from the uneven surface of the slate. Finally, after I've finished cleaning the floor, I let it sit for 24 to 48 hours, then apply a second coat of sealer with a sponge. On a large floor, I usually use a pump sprayer on the final coat.

Tom Meehan is a second-generation tile installer who has been installing tile for more than 35 years. Tom lives with his wife, Lane, and their four sons in Harwich, Massachusetts, where they own Cape Cod Tileworks.

Sources

Schlüter Company
800-472-4588
www.schluter.com
Ditra and expansion joints

C.H. Hanson Tool Co.
800-827-3398
www.chhanson.com
3-4-5 aSquare

Miracle Sealants Company
800-350-1901
www.miraclesealants.com
Miracle Sealants Porous Plus

The Tile Council of America
864-646-8453
www.tileusa.com

Glass Tile

■ BY TOM MEEHAN

It has been used for centuries, but until recently, glass tile was relegated to museums and specialty shops. Today, it comes in an array of styles, from iridescent mosaics to luminous squares of recycled and sandblasted beer bottles (see "A Peek Into the World of Glass Tile" on pp. 168–169). Tile shops like mine see glass-tile sales double every year. However, lots of folks are in for a shock if they try to install it like

ceramic tile: The thinset and its application are different; the paper backing for small tiles is stuck to the front, not to the back of the tiles; and timing becomes an important part of the job.

Layout Needs Room to Move

On this particular job, the shower area was to be covered with 1-in. tiles grouped into 12-in.-sq. sheets. When I work with small tiles, I try to make sure that the backerboard is smooth and flat; any imperfections will show as bumps in the tile. This phenomenon is especially true with glass tiles, which catch the light even more than ceramic or stone. Once I've installed the backerboard, I seal the joints between the sheets with thinset and mesh tape, and then smooth any bumps with a steel floating trowel and thinset. The thinset should set overnight before the tile is installed.

When laying out a back wall, don't be tempted to squeeze the sheets together so that you can get a full tile and avoid cutting. Believe it or not, glass tiles expand and contract with changes in temperature, much more so than ceramic tiles. Direct sunlight can heat tiles enough to make them move. If tiles are too tight, any movement can make them pop off the wall or crack—or even crack the backerboard. I try to leave ¼ in. of space in each corner; intersecting walls hide the gap.

I begin the layout with a level horizontal line halfway up the back wall, equivalent to an even course of tile, which in this case worked out to be 48 in. from the top of the tub. This horizontal line serves not only as a reference for spacing but also, as you'll see later, marks the extent of the first round of applying the glass tile. Next, I measure up to determine the width of the row at the ceiling. Anything over a half piece works well, and I can adjust the cut to make up the difference when the ceiling is uneven.

Thinset? Make Mine Extra-Sticky

Because it's vitreous, glass doesn't absorb liquid like ceramic tile, and it requires a higher grade of acrylic or latex-modified thinset to bond to the backerboard. Most glass-tile manufacturers specify what brands of thinset to use. Because the tile often is translucent, the thinset should be white; gray mixes darken the tile's color. Any pattern the trowel leaves in the thinset will show through, too, so the thinset must be spread and leveled with a ³⁄₁₆-in. V-notch trowel, and then smoothed out (see "Troweling" on the facing page).

I start laying the tile sheets from the level line, and then work down rather than working with a full sheet off the tub. If the tub is out of level, it's easier to adjust the cuts as measured from the course above. Once I press the sheets into the thinset and finish the half wall, I use a block of wood and a hammer to bed the tile fully and evenly into the thinset. You also can use a beater block (a wooden block padded on one side with a piece of rubber, available from most tile distributors) and a rubber mallet. I make any cuts with a wet saw (see the bottom photo on p. 166) fitted with a diamond blade; a pair of tile nippers is handy to make minor adjustments in a cut.

Timing Is Crucial When Removing Paper Facing

The main reason I don't install too much glass tile at one time is that while the thinset is wet, I need to move individual tiles and erase any pattern inadvertently created by the 12-in. tile sheets. But first I have to peel off the paper facing carefully so that I don't disturb the majority of tiles.

After waiting 15 to 20 minutes for the thinset to bond, I wet the paper with a

Troweling

Many glass tiles are translucent, so you need to use white thinset because gray will show through and darken the tile. With a $\frac{3}{16}$-in. V-notch trowel, roughly distribute the thinset over a small area (photo 1). Even out the material using the trowel's notched edge (photo 2), then smooth the ridges (photo 3) so that they won't show through the tile.

Even out the thinset.

1

Spread thinset on the wall.

3

Smooth the ridges.

Setting

Many varieties of small glass field tile are held together in sheets by a paper facing on the front (photo 1) rather than a mesh fabric on the back. (Mesh on the back might be visible through the translucent material.) To make a wall of tile appear unified and not look like a grid of 12-in. squares, the paper must be removed and individual tiles adjusted to mask the pattern.

The trick lies in waiting for the thinset to become tacky; in normal conditions, this might be 15 minutes or 20 minutes. If the thinset is allowed to dry beyond that time, say an hour, the bond becomes more fragile, and more tiles will pull off with the paper. If the thinset is left to dry overnight, the bond sets, and the tile will be impossible to adjust.

The author first wets the paper with a sponge dampened with warm water (photo 2); after a few minutes, the water-based glue softens, and the paper can be peeled off gently (photo 3).

During the process of peeling the paper, individual tiles will fall off occasionally (photo 4). A quick coat of thinset on the tile's back is enough to set it back in place.

Simple jig for cutting small tile

Cut with a wet saw, small glass tiles often are difficult to hold and cut accurately. The author makes an L-shaped cut in a larger piece of tile and uses it as a jig that holds the smaller tiles in line with the sawblade.

1 Set the tile.

3 Peel carefully.

2 Dampen the paper.

4 Make an easy fix.

Grouting

Each tile manufacturer specifies what type of grout to use on a particular tile. After the grout is spread (photo 1) and has set up for about 20 minutes, the author wipes away the excess with cheesecloth or paper towels (photo 2). A sponge dampened with clean water (photo 3) works well to clean any residue from the tile.

Wipe the excess.

Pack the seams.

Clean the tile.

sponge and warm water. After a minute or so, the paper can be pulled off slowly, downward at an angle. One or two tiles may pop off, but that's no big deal; I just stick them back in place with a dab of thinset.

The trickiest part of this process is that the timing varies according to the room's temperature and humidity. Heat and dry conditions make the thinset bond faster and give me less time to work, so I start to check the bond in an inconspicuous place after about 10 minutes. If the tiles move around too easily as I peel off a bit of paper, I know that I should wait a few more minutes.

Once the paper is off, the glass tiles must be examined to make sure none has slipped.

Never wait until the next day to remove the paper; the tiles have to be examined and straightened while the thinset is fresh (see "Setting" on the facing page).

When Grouting, Less Water Is Better

After the thinset has bonded fully for 48 hours, the tile must be washed to prepare it for grouting. I use a nylon-bristle brush and a sponge with warm water to clean any residue or paper backing from the surface of the tile. I use a utility knife to remove any excess thinset in the joints, but I'm careful when doing so; glass tile scratches easily.

A Peek into the World of Glass Tile

Glass tile is versatile stuff; it's available in styles that range from clear to opaque, from glossy and iridescent to the eroded look of beach glass.

Colors range from gaudy lollipop primaries to muted earth tones and just about every shade in between. Commonly seen in sheets of 1-in. squares, glass tile now is made in sizes that approximate ceramic tiles (2-in., 4-in., and even 12-in. squares), as well as rectangles, textured borders, and tiny mosaics. And like ceramics, it can be used on walls, counters, and floors, although glass tiles used on floors should have a matte finish or texture that makes them slip-proof.

One big factor to consider: Glass is more likely to show scratches than ceramics or stone; finishes applied to the tile are susceptible to scratches, too.

Texture with a variety of color

These 4-in.-sq., clear-glass tiles from Architectural Glass (see "Sources" on p. 170) have textured faces and ribbed backs; a glaze bonded to the tile backs gives them their color. The company also offers a higher-end integral color tile and custom designs.

Earth tones in recycled glass

Made from 100% recycled content, Bedrock tiles (see "Sources" on p. 170) are available in many sizes, from 2-in. squares to 5-in. x 10-in. rectangles to hexagonal shapes. Finish can be glossy or matte, but the color is integral and ranges from clear to solidly opaque.

Grouting glass tiles is not difficult, but again, it's different from grouting ceramic tile. Some manufacturers specify sanded or non-sanded grout; here, I used a recommended sanded grout in a color that complemented the tile. After I spread the grout on the walls, I let it set for about 20 minutes; the wait is longer than for ceramic tile because the glass tile doesn't absorb moisture from the grout.

Before starting to clean with water, I use cheesecloth or paper towels to rub down the walls to get rid of any extra grout and to fill in any voids between the tiles. This dry method also lets me clean the surface without adding any extra moisture that might dilute the grout.

Once the tile is wiped down, I go back over it with clean water and a damp sponge

Solid colors in mosaics

Hakatai (see "Sources" on p. 170) sells mesh-backed mosaics (instead of paper-faced) in ¾-in. and 1-in. sizes in many opaque and solid colors. They also offer 2-in. squares of clear glass with color fired onto the tile back and irregularly shaped pebbles.

Broad palette of recycled color

Sandhill (see "Sources" on p. 170) makes mosaic, field, and specialty tile from 100% recycled glass in 36 different shades of integral color, glossy or matte. They also offer custom border and mosaic designs.

Iridescence

Oceanside Glasstile® (see "Sources" on p. 170) offers a variety of tile ranging from 1-in.-sq. mosaics to 5-in. x 5-in. field tiles, specialty borders, and decorative single tiles. Many feature a metallic glaze that's applied to the surface of the tile.

to do a finer cleaning and to reduce any topical film. Less water is better. As in any grouting job, it's important to strike corners or intersections of wall and tile with a trowel or putty knife to make sure these joints are tight and neat. Once everything is set and a slight film has developed over the tile, I use a rag to bring the glass tile to a shine. I try not to wait more than 15 minutes after sponging; any longer, and the film starts to set up and becomes too hard to remove easily (see "Grouting" on p. 167).

Simple Tip for Grouting Tile

Instead of using a specialized edge tile, the author sometimes runs the field tile to the wall edge and smooths any sharp edges with a diamond-impregnated pad.

Sources

Architectural Glass Inc.
845-733-4720
www.architecturalglassinc.com

Bedrock Industries
877-283-7625
www.bedrockindustries.com

Hakatai Enterprises Inc.
888-667-2429
www.hakatai.com

Miracle Sealants Company
800-350-1901
www.miraclesealants.com
511 Impregnator

Oceanside Glasstile
760-929-4000
www.glasstile.com

Sandhill Industries
208-345-6508
www.sandhillind.com

Cleaning and Sealing Are Just as Important as Thinset and Grout

A day or two after grouting, I smooth exposed tile edges with a diamond-abrasive pad, and then clean the tile with a commercial tile cleaner. I wet down the walls before applying the cleaner and also protect any chrome or brass plumbing fixtures with tape and plastic bags. Rather than use stronger cleaners that might compromise the grout, I use a fine, nylon scrubbing pad to clean off heavy grout residue. I always give the walls a double rinse to flush away any cleaner residue.

Sealing grout is simple and should not be overlooked; it helps keep grout lines from absorbing mildew and other stains. I use a wet, clean cloth rag and apply a double coat of sealer on the grout and tile as well. I then towel off the wall with a dry rag. I used Miracle Sealants 511 Impregnator (see "Sources" at left) on this project. One key to sealing walls is to start from the bottom and work up from floor to ceiling to avoid streaking. Once the sealer is dry, glass-tile maintenance is minimal; I use dish soap and water to clean it on a regular basis.

Tom Meehan is a second-generation tile installer who has been installing tile for more than 35 years. Tom lives with his wife, Lane, and their four sons in Harwich, Massachusetts, where they own Cape Cod Tileworks.

Tiling with Limestone

■ BY TOM MEEHAN

My wife, Lane, and I own a tile store on Cape Cod, so I've gotten used to seeing tile of many different colors, shapes, and materials all in the same room. But I've never met a homeowner who wanted to turn a bathroom into a tile showroom. I did come close recently when I tiled a bathroom that combined striking black marble; gray granite; tumbled marble; and a large, colorful hand-painted ceramic mural. The unifying element that made this unlikely combination successful was limestone tile.

Sort the Tiles before You Mix the Mortar

As an experienced tile installer, I had the dream job of integrating all these different types of tile with limestone in a single room. Limestone, which can be fairly soft and porous, is usually a breeze to work with and has subtle, earthy tones that form a perfect complement to almost any type or color of material (see "Limestone's Origins: Fossils, Coral, and Seashells" below).

Because the color of limestone can vary from tile to tile and from box to box, I begin by opening boxes and checking the tiles for differences in shade or slight veining that might make one tile stand out from the rest.

The differences are usually subtle, but a misplaced tile in a different shade can stick out.

As I went through the boxes of limestone tiles for this bathroom, I culled some tiles that had slightly different shades or that had chipped corners. I also came across some tiles with nice crystalline veins that I set aside to give large open areas, such as the floor or the shower walls, a monolithic look. Out of the 550 sq. ft. of limestone tile that I installed in this bathroom, only about 20 or 30 tiles were irregular in color or badly chipped. These tiles were set aside for cuts, and tiles with off colors were relegated to an inconspicuous closet floor.

To add interest to the layout, we decided to run the tiles diagonally on the horizontal areas (tub deck and main floor). The diagonal pattern contrasted the square layout of the wainscoting and the shower walls. For the floor, I figured that a 6-in. border (in black marble) would allow me to use more full tiles and fewer small pieces in the field.

To enhance the diagonal layout, I positioned 3-in. black-marble inserts at the intersection of every fourth tile. A pattern of inserts done this way is called a clipped-corner pattern because the corners of the intersecting tiles are cut off to accommodate the insert. I centered the floor pattern in the

Limestone's Origins: Fossils, Coral, and Seashells

Look at limestone under a microscope, and you'll see coral, seashells, and the skeletons of sea creatures that accumulated over eons in the sediment on the ocean floor. Millions of years ago, the surface of the earth was changing dramatically. Mountains were thrust up out of the oceans, and the sediment on the ocean floor turned into limestone. Some of that limestone encountered tremendous geological heat and pressure, crystallizing and transforming it into marble.

Like marble, limestone occurs in a wide variety of textures and colors from grays, greens, and reds to almost pure white. Far and away the most common color of limestone tile is a sandy beige like the tile used here. Even so, a single tile can have specific areas of contrasting color, and often you can see the full outline of a seashell or fossil in limestone's richly textured surface.

Cutting and Installing Limestone

A wet saw is the best tool for cutting limestone, but installation is similar to regular tile.

Wet-saw jig from a tile scrap. A discarded tile cut at a 45-degree angle and clamped to the wet saw's sliding table streamlines cutting tiles for a diagonal layout.

Buttered back for better adhesion. Because of limestone's porous nature, the back of every tile receives a thin layer of mortar, a process known as buttering, which ensures sound attachment for each tile.

No special mortar for limestone. After the backs are buttered, the limestone tiles are set in the same latex-modified mortar used for many other types of tile. The lighter color was chosen because darker mortars can darken the limestone permanently.

area that would be seen first, in front of the raised-panel tub-enclosure face.

Another layout concern was the long exposed wall that holds the main door to the bathroom. To catch another full diagonal tile, I increased the border along that wall to about 6½ in. My objective was to give the appearance that the room was built to the size and dimension of the limestone tile.

The layout of the walls was relatively simple. Because the floor tiles ran diagonally, the walls and floor did not have to line up. I made it a point to avoid small cuts whenever possible and to put the fuller-cut tiles in obvious places such as inside corners. The mural was centered on the wall above the tub to give the feeling of looking out a big limestone and ceramic window at Cape Cod's scenic landscape.

Shaping Limestone

imestone can be worked almost like wood, taking shapes and finished edges with ease. But unlike highly polished marble, a light sanding is all limestone needs before it is ready to be installed.

Cut tiles are glued temporarily to the template. After the tiles are cut, the author glues them to the template. Having the tiles aligned the way they will be installed makes it easier to keep the edge shape consistent.

Arched door trim starts with a plywood template. After scribing the arch of the shower entry onto a piece of plywood and adding the top edge of the tile trim, that shape is transferred to the limestone.

A grinder roughs out the bullnose. An abrasive pad on an electric grinder fairs the curve of the arch and rounds over the tiles. A quick pass with 80-grit and then 120-grit sandpaper gets the tile ready for installation.

A Wet Saw Is Indispensable

Working with limestone is similar to working with polished marble. However, marble is much less forgiving and is usually set in a perfect plane with no grout joint. But in most cases, limestone can look better with a fine grout joint. On this job, I left a ⅛-in. joint between the tiles.

Because limestone is part of a geological formation (sedimentary rock), it should be cut only with a wet saw equipped with a diamond-edge blade (see "Cutting and Installing Limestone" on p. 173). I precut as many pieces as possible, especially when the tile is being installed in a diagonal pattern.

As with most tiles, limestone seems to bond best either to a good cement backerboard or to a cement-and-sand-based mud job in wet areas such as the shower and tub. Limestone also bonds well to drywall in areas where water isn't a concern. I did a mud job on the shower floor and used backerboard for the shower walls and for the tub deck running up the walls a foot or so. For the rest of the wall work, I installed the limestone over the mildew-resistant drywall on the walls after priming the drywall with a skim coat of thinset the day before installing the tiles.

One often-overlooked characteristic of limestone is its translucence. Regular gray thinset has a tendency to darken the light-colored limestone, so I always install the tile with white latex-modified thinset. For this job I used Laticrete 253, a polymer-modified thinset mortar that mixes with water.

I spread the mortar for these limestone tiles with a ⅜-in. notched spreading trowel. Before installing each tile, I buttered the back with a thin layer of thinset. This step may be slightly overkill, but it is cheap insurance for achieving a 100 percent bond when the tile is set in place.

The arch goes up. Once the tiles are shaped and smoothed, they are installed on the wall, leaving the proper spacing for an attractive grout joint.

Limestone Can Be Shaped with a Grinder and Sandpaper

When I'm installing an outside corner with ceramic tile, I have to order special tiles to achieve the bullnose edge. With stone tiles such as marble and limestone, edges can be carved or ground right into the edge of regular tiles. With polished marble, that edge has to be polished with a series of abrasive disks that get progressively finer. However, with limestone, once the bullnose edge is roughed out, I just go over it with 80-grit sandpaper to fine-tune the shape and then 120-grit sandpaper to smooth the finish. If I go any finer with the sandpaper, I have to be careful not to make the edge more polished than the tile itself.

One challenge in tile work made easy with limestone is forming tiles for an arched opening like the one I did over the shower entry in this bathroom. The first step was scribing the arched opening onto plywood for a template. Then I set a compass at 4 in. and paralleled my scribe line to form the arch. After cutting out the arch template, I traced the shape onto three pieces of limestone (see "Shaping Limestone" on p. 174).

It was easy to follow the outside radius of the arch with the wet saw, but the inside radius was challenging. I sawed over to the inside-radius line and removed the bulk of the waste. I then used my grinder to cut to the line.

The top of the radius still had to be bull-nosed. The best way to put an even edge on a series of tiles is to join them together in the same order as they will be installed. For a square edge such as an outside corner of a wall, I just line up the tiles against a straightedge on the worktable and mold them as a single entity.

The arch, however, was a more formidable task. I began by gluing the pieces of limestone to the plywood template. I used a glue called Akemi® (see "Sources" on the facing page), a quick-setting two-part polyester used to join stone to stone. In that capacity it forms a tenacious bond, but because I was gluing to plywood, I was able to break the

Seal Limestone before and after Grouting

A coat of sealer before grouting helps prevent the porous limestone from sucking moisture out of the grout as it cures. The final coat protects the tile from bathroom moisture.

The first coat of sealer. Sealing before the grout is spread keeps the tiles from absorbing the liquid in the grout and keeps the grout from staining the tiles.

The final coat of sealer. When all the tile is installed and grouted, a second coat of sealer is applied over the entire tiled surface. Sealer keeps the limestone from staining.

Protecting limestone from dark grouts. Here, the light-colored limestone has been masked off while black grout is applied to the marble border.

bond and chip off the glue when I was finished shaping. Next, I used an electric grinder to round over the top edge of the arch to form half of a bullnose. After I finished the edge with sandpaper, the tiles were installed with the preshaped edge, forming a continuous curve (see the photo on p. 175).

Seal Twice, Grout Once

Cleaning and sealing the limestone before grouting are musts. At this stage, limestone should be sealed with a coat of an impregnator sealer to protect it from staining and to act as a grout release before grouting (see "Seal Limestone before and after Grouting" on the facing page). Manufacturers suggest testing the sealer on a small area of stone first. A good impregnator should not darken stone but rather leave stone in its natural state when it dries. I try to seal the edges of the tile as well so that the porous limestone doesn't suck the moisture out of the grout and cause it to cure prematurely.

I used the sealer, Miracle Sealants' 511 Porous Plus (see "Sources" at right). I usually apply the sealer with a foam brush and then wipe down the tile with a clean rag. This sealer gives off organic vapors, so if you're not installing the limestone in a well-ventilated area, I recommend wearing a respirator.

I grouted the limestone with a latex-modified floor grout made by TEC (see "Sources" at right). For these ⅛-in.-wide grout joints, I chose a sanded grout. Once the tile had been sealed and dried 24 hours, I grouted in pretty much the same way I do for most other tiles, raking the grout in diagonal strokes across the grout joints to ensure that they get completely filled. When I'm grouting limestone, though, I try not to spread or cover more than 40 sq. ft. to 50 sq. ft. at a time. If any places in the grout joint did not get sealer, the grout could cure too quickly, making it difficult to work and also reducing its strength.

A Cleanup before the Final Sealer

I waited two or three days to let the grout cure completely and then cleaned the tile thoroughly with a neutral-pH cleaner. Your local tile store can steer you toward several different cleaners. I then let the tile dry for a week or more, depending on the humidity, before applying the final coat of sealer. Some sealer manufacturers recommend that you wait 30 days before sealing to make sure all the moisture is released from the stone. Unlike other sealers, an impregnator sealer allows the tile to breathe and to release its vapors after the sealer is applied.

The French limestone in this bathroom is highly porous, so I doubled the final coat of sealer on the floor and tripled it on the tub deck and in the shower. When sealing shower walls, I start at the bottom and work my way up to prevent sealer from streaking. I also make sure that I don't leave puddles of sealer on flat surfaces. Pooling sealer can darken and glaze over limestone.

The black grout that I used on the marble border can seriously stain the limestone. So after the limestone is sealed, I mask it off before spreading the black grout.

Should you discover scratches or marks that won't disappear with regular cleaning, those areas can be hit lightly with 120-grit or 220-grit sandpaper. Once I have sanded a tile to remove a mark, I then reapply a coat of sealer.

Tom Meehan is a second-generation tile installer who has been installing tile for more than 35 years. Tom lives with his wife, Lane, and their four sons in Harwich, Massachusetts, where they own Cape Cod Tileworks.

Sources

Akemi
www.akemi.de/en/company

Laticrete International Inc.
800-243-4788
www.laticrete.com
Laticrete 253

Miracle Sealants Company
800-350-1901
www.miraclesealants.com
511 Porous Plus

TEC
800-TEC-9002
www.tecspecialty.com
Floor grout

A Mural in a Field of Stone

The crown jewel of this bathroom is a hand-painted ceramic-tile mural by Pat Wehrman of the Dodge Lane Potter Group in Sonora, California. The mural—done in three sections—depicts a salt marsh with cattails and great blue herons, the same view someone is likely to have looking out the large bay window over the tub. Even though the individual pieces in each section were large, the mural went together like one of the jigsaw puzzles my sons love to play with.

I'm always extra careful handling the pieces of a mural. If a piece gets lost or broken, it is nearly impossible to replace it with one that will match the original both in size and in color.

Each section of the mural came with a map to help us reconstruct it accurately (photo 1). First, James Mahony, my assistant, dry-fit all the sections together on a large sheet of plywood, while I put layout lines on the wall.

Next, I set the limestone tile on the wall up to where the mural began. Starting at the lower right-hand corner, I worked up and across each section of the mural. I set the mural tiles in the same white thinset I used for the limestone (photo 2). Because of the irregular shapes and sizes of the mural pieces, I spread the thinset with the same 3/8-in. by 3/8-in. notched trowel. As each section was completed, I moved the pieces with my fingertips until the grout joints were perfect. A few strategically placed plastic wedges helped keep the pieces from drifting back.

The final installation step was adding the limestone frame around each section (photo 3). The limestone was sealed, grouted, and sealed again. Magically, as the limestone around the mural dried, the subtle colors in the stone enhanced and magnified all the hues in the hand-painted glaze of the mural.

Assembling a ceramic jigsaw puzzle. With the help of a paper map provided by the artist, the installer lays out the ceramic-tile mural carefully on a sheet of plywood (photo 1). After it is laid out, the mural is assembled from its lower corner; the installer works up and over until each section is completed (photo 2). When all the sections are set in place and framed with limestone, a final rinse and wipe down removes excess mortar from the hand-painted ceramic surface (photo 3).

Replacing a Broken Tile

■ BY JANE AEON

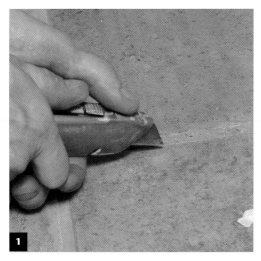

Isolate the victim. To keep the neighboring tiles intact, the first step is to score the grout lines with a utility knife. A few light passes do the trick.

Protection is prevention. Before cutting, it's a good idea to mask off any nearby cabinets or furniture with plastic and tape. On the floor, angle brackets taped to the surrounding tiles protect them from inadvertent slips of the grinder's blade.

It was bound to happen. The new floors have been finished for less than a week, and someone already has dropped a hammer on the kitchen's tile floor. Unless the tile guy is still on the job, you're either going to wait a long time or fix it yourself.

Luckily, it's a fairly easy fix, as long as you use the right technique. Although you can use a hammer and an old chisel to break out the damaged tile, this technique can be risky. Within grout joints tighter than 3/16 in., hammer blows can chip or crack adjacent tiles. Hammering also can pulverize the substrate beneath the damaged tile.

Occasionally, I use a hole saw to cut out the center portion of a cracked tile. This technique is good for removing soft-bodied tile. It's usually a slow process, but I'm left with a hole in the tile that makes it easy to pry with the tip of a chisel or a screwdriver.

My preferred technique, however, is to use an angle grinder outfitted with a 4-in. diamond blade made by Pearl Abrasive (see "Sources" on p. 183) and a shop vacuum. This technique is good for thick, soft-bodied tiles such as saltillo, but it works on others as well. The tile must be larger than 4 in., or there won't be room for a 4-in. grinder blade.

Diagonal cuts open up the tile. With both hands firmly holding the grinder, the author carefully plunges the blade into the tile's center and cuts diagonally, then along the tile's sides. A helper holds the vacuum hose to catch the dusty exhaust.

A junky tool still has its uses. Using a hammer and an old chisel or putty knife, the author works from the outside toward the tile's center, carefully prying out the pieces.

4

Basically, the trick is first to isolate the tile from neighboring tiles by removing the surrounding grout line, then carefully break the tile into pieces and remove it. Using a grinder can be messy unless you keep a vacuum nozzle trained on the dust stream. I mask off any surrounding cabinet faces or furniture, and also protect neighboring tiles with sheet metal or plywood in case I overcut. I mask off myself as well, by donning safety glasses, a dust mask, and my hearing protection.

I start by making diagonal cuts, then make separate cuts that run parallel to the edges. The parallel cuts along the tile edges make it possible to position a chisel from the edge of a tile facing in so that the neighboring tile is not damaged. This technique is good for removing tiles with tight joints, like marble. There's also a cordless 3⅜-in. saw made by Makita with a slightly smaller diamond blade that comes in handy; I also use a Dremel tool fitted with a small

Sources

Dremel
800-437-3635
www.dremel.com

Makita
800-462-5482
www.makita.com

Pearl Abrasive Co.
800-969-5561
www.pearlabrasive.com

Make a clear space. After the tile is removed, all old thinset and grout are scraped from the substrate, which is then vacuumed clean.

Back to square one, again. After making sure the replacement tile fits, the author mixes a small batch of thinset, trowels it into the space (photo 6), and sets the tile. After the thinset dries, the tile can be grouted.

#7134 diamond-point bit in the corners where the grinder can't reach (see "Sources" at top right).

Once the tile is removed, I scrape out any remaining thinset and vacuum the substrate. With fresh thinset and a new tile, the job is finished, except for the grouting work.

Jane Aeon is a tile contractor in Berkeley, California, and Oklahoma City, Oklahoma.

CREDITS

All photos are courtesy of *Fine Homebuilding* magazine (*FHb*) © The Taunton Press, Inc., except as noted below:

p. iii: Photo by Charles Bickford (*FHb*); p. iv: (left photo) Scott Gibson (*FHb*), (right photo) courtesy © Lindsay Meehan; p. 1: (left and right photos) Charles Bickford (*FHb*)

p. 4: Tiling a Tub Surround by Michael Byrne, issue 92. All photos by Kevin Ireton (*FHb*) except for photos on
p. 9 by Krystan S. Doerfler (*FHb*).

p. 15: Upgrading to a Tile Shower by Tom Meehan, issue 160. All photos by Roe A. Osborn (*FHb*) except right photo on p. 15 and top photo on p. 18 by Charles Bickford (*FHb*), bottom photos on p. 18 and photo on
p. 19 by Krystan S. Doerfler (*FHb*), and right photos on p. 21 courtesy © Lasco Bathware. Drawing by Dan Thorton (*FHb*).

p. 24: Installing a Shower Niche by Jane Aeon, issue 196. All photos by Rob Yagid (*FHb*) except photo on
p. 29 by Krystan S. Doerfler (*FHb*).

p. 30: Tiling a Shower with Marble by Tom Meehan, issue 98. Photos by Jefferson Kolle (*FHb*).

p. 38: Glass-Block Shower on a Curve by Tom Meehan, issue 200. All photos by Justin Fink except photo on
p. 38 courtesy © Tom Meehan and left photos on p. 42 by Krystan S. Doerfler (*FHb*).

p. 45: Tiling a Bathroom Floor by Dennis Hourany, issue 124. Photos by Scott Gibson (*FHb*); Drawing by Dan Thorton (*FHb*).

p. 54: A Sloping Floor for a Barrier-Free Bath by Tom Meehan, issue 185. All photos by Roe A. Osborn (*FHb*) except photo on p. 59 (bottom left), p. 60 (left photos) and p. 61 (top and middle photos) by Krystan S. Doerfler (*FHb*). Drawings courtesy © Clark Barre.

p. 64: Installing a Leakproof Shower Plan by Tom Meehan, issue 141. All photos by Roe A. Osborn (*FHb*) except photos on p. 69 courtesy © Tom and Lane Meehan. Drawings by Rick Daskam (FHb).

p. 72: Bubble Bath by Maria Lapiana, issue SIP 20. Photos by Charles Miller (*FHb*); Drawings by Martha Garstang Hill (FHb).

p. 78: Bathroom-Tile Design by Lynn Hopkins, issue SIP 20. Drawings by Martha Garstang Hill (*FHb*).

p. 82: Details from Great Bathrooms. Photo on p. 82 (left), p. 83 (right photos), p. 84 (top left and bottom left photos), p. 85 (left and top right photos) by Brian Pontolilo (*FHb*); p. 83 (left), p. 84 (top right and bottom right photos), by Charles Miller (*FHb*); p. 85 (bottom right photo) by Debra Judge Silber (*FHb*).

p. 86: Putting Tile to Work in a Kitchen by Lane Meehan, issue 127. Photos by Roe A. Osborn (*FHb*) except photo on p. 87 courtesy © Andrea Rugg, p. 88 courtesy © Judi Rutz, p. 89 photos by Krystan S. Doerfler (*FHb*). Drawings by Paul Perreault (*FHb*).

p. 95: Tiling a Kitchen Counter by Dennis Hourany, issue 120. All photos by Scott Gibson (*FHb*) except photos on p. 103 by Krystan S. Doerfler (*FHb*).

p. 108: Tiling Over A Laminate Counter by David Hart, issue 130. Photos by Charles Bickford (*FHb*).

p. 113: Tiling a Backsplash by Tom Meehan, issue 167. Photos courtesy © Lindsay Meehan.

p. 118: Details from a Great Kitchen. Photo on p. 118 (left), p. 119, p. 120 (top left and right) by Brian Pontolilo (*FHb*); p. 120 (bottom left), p. 121 (bottom left and bottom right) by Charles Bickford (*FHb*); p. 118 (right) by Charles Miller (*FHb*); p. 121 (top) Justin Fink (*FHb*).

p. 122: Buying or Renting Tile Saws by Tom Meehan, issue 132. All photos by Justin Fink (*FHb*) except photos on p. 123 and p. 125 (bottom right) courtesy © Nat Rea; p. 128 (bottom) by Rodney Diaz (*FHb*).

p. 132: Cutting Ceramic Tile by David Hart, issue 148. Photos by Charles Bickford (*FHb*).

p. 140: Grouting Tile by David Hart, issue 138. Photos by Charles Bickford (*FHb*); Drawings by Rick Daskam (*FHb*).

p. 148: A Fearless Approach to Epoxy Grout by Tom Meehan, issue 208. All photos by Justin Fink (*FHb*) except photos on p. 149 by Dan Thorton (FHb); photos on p. 152 by Krystan S. Doerfler (*FHb*).

p. 153: A New Way to Tile a Big Floor by Tom Meehan, issue 173. Photos by Roe A. Osborn (*FHb*); Drawings by Chuck Lockhart (*FHb*).

p. 163: Glass Tile by Tom Meehan, issue 161. All photos by Charles Bickford (FHb) except photos on pp. 168–169 by Dan Thorton (*FHb*).

p. 171: Tiling with Limestone by Tom Meehan, issue 118. Photos by Roe A. Osborn (*FHb*).

p. 180: Replacing a Broken Tile by Jane Aeon, issue 168. Photos by Charles Bickford (*FHb*).

INDEX